Dog Poems

A Heartwarming Collection of Poems About Man's Best Friend

Thomas Genther

© 2009 by GSL Publishing
All rights reserved.

Chattanooga, Tennessee, USA

Printed in the United States of America.

Preface

Matthew Arnold, explaining why those were his most popular poems which dealt with his canine pets, Geist, Kaiser, and Max, said that while comparatively few loved poetry, nearly everyone loved dogs.

The literature of the Anglo-Saxon is rich in tributes to the dog, as becomes a race which beyond any other has understood and developed its four-footed companions. Canine heroes whose intelligence and faithfulness our prose writers have celebrated start to the memory in scores—Bill Sykes's white shadow, which refused to be separated from its master even by death; Rab, savagely devoted; the immortal Bob, "son of battle"—true souls all, with hardly a villain among them for artistic contrast. Even Red Wull, the killer, we admire for his courage and loyalty.

Within these covers is a selection from a large body of dog verse. It is a selection made on the principle of human appeal. Dialect, and the poems of the earlier writers whose diction strikes oddly on our modern ears, have for the most part been omitted. The place of such classics as may be missed is filled by that vagrant verse which is often most truly the flower of inspiration.

Acknowledgements

To the loving memory of every reader's
dog's both past and present.

Contents

I **Puppyhood** 1
   We Meet At Morn 2
   The Lost Puppy 3
   A Laugh in Church 5
   Treasures 6
   That There Long Dog 7
   My Friend 8
   Ted 10
   Little Lost Pup 11
   My Brindle Bull-Terrier 12
   Lauth 13
   The Drowned Spaniel 14

II **The Human Relationship** 16
   Cluny 17
   The Best Friend 18
   My Dog and I 19
   My Gentleman 20
   The Dead Boy's Portrait and His Dog 21
   Advice to a Dog Painter 23
   Mercy's Reward 24
   Beau and the Water Lily 26
   Petronius 28
   My Dog 29
   Charity's Eye 31
   To Blanco 32
   The Ould Hound 33
   The Miser's Only Friend 35
   Poor Dog Try 37
   My Comforter 38

The Little White Dog		39
The Irish Greyhound		40
The Vagabonds		41
In Cineam		46
Old Mathew's Dog		46
A Dog and A Man		49
Rover-Dog		50
Horse, Dog and Man		52
The Best Dog		54
Caesar, King Edward's Dog		55
Just Our Dog		56
Ragged Rover		58
The Flush, My Dog		59
Frances		65
To My Setter, Scout		67
Why Strik'st Thou Me?		69
Consolation		70
Argus		71
Chained in the Yard		72
Why the Dog's Nose is Cold		73
Dog Language		75
A Dog's Loyalty		76
III **The Dog in Action**		77
Told to the Missionary		78
The Dog of the Louvre		82
The Chase		85
The Under Dog		86
The Shepherd and His Dog		87
Beth Gelert		88
The Flag and the Faithful		91
A Guardian at the Gate		92
A Tale of the Reign of Terror		93

	An Elegy on the Death of a Mad Dog	99
	The Fusiliers' Dog	101
	Fidelity	104
	Shepherd Dog of the Pyrenees	106
	The Dog Under the Wagon	108
	Sal's Tower and My Trouser	110
	Rover in Church	112
IV	**The Dog's Hereafter**	114
	Billy	115
	The Bond	116
	To a Dog	117
	Canine Immortality	118
	A Friendly Welcome	120
	Exemplary Nick	120
	The Difference	121
	Laddie	121
	A Dog's Epitaph	123
	The Passing of a Dog	124
	My Dog	125
	Jack	126
	In Memory of Don	127
	Roderick Dhu	128
	Questions	130
	His Epitaph	130
	In Memoriam	131
	Questions	133
	Our Dog Jack	133
	Tory, a Puppy	134
	On an Irish Retriever	135
	A Retriever's Epitaph	136

1

Puppyhood

   What other nature yours than of a child
Whose dumbness finds a voice mighty to call,
In wordless pity, to the souls of all,
Whose lives I turn to profit, and whose mute
And constant friendship links the man and brute?

WE MEET AT MORN

Still half in dream, upon the stair I hear
A patter coming nearer and more near,
And then upon my chamber door
A gentle tapping,
For dogs, though proud, are poor,
And if a tail will do to give command
Why use a hand?
And after that a cry, half sneeze, half yapping,
And next a scuffle on the passage floor,
And then I know the creature lies to watch
Until the noiseless maid will lift the latch.
And like a spring
That gains its power by being tightly stayed,
The impatient thing
Into the room
Its whole glad heart doth fling,
And ere the gloom
Melts into light, and window blinds are rolled,
I hear a bounce upon the bed,
I feel a creeping toward me--a soft head,
And on my face
A tender nose, and cold--
This is the way, you know, that dogs embrace--
And on my hand, like sun-warmed rose-leaves flung,
The least faint flicker of the warmest tongue
--And so my dog and I have met and sworn
Fresh love and fealty for another morn.

-HARDWICKE DRUMMOND RAWNSLEY.

THE LOST PUPPY

Say! little pup,
　　What's up?
Your tail is down
　And out of sight
Between your legs;
　Why, that ain't right.
　　Little pup,
　　　Brace up!

Say! little pup,
　　Look up!
Don't hang your head
　And look so sad,
You're all mussed up,
　But you ain't mad.
　　Little pup,
　　　Cheer up!

Say! little pup,
　　Stir up!
Is that a string
　Around your tail?
And was it fast
　To a tin pail?
　　Little pup,
　　　Git up.

Say! little pup,

Dog Poems

   Talk up.
Were those bad boys
  All after you,
With sticks and stones,
  And tin cans, too?
    Little pup,
      Speak up!

Say! little pup,
    Stand up!
Let's look at you;
  You'd be all right
If you was scrubbed
  And shined up bright.
    Little pup,
      Jump up!

Say! little pup,
    Bark up!
Let's hear your voice.
  Say, you're a brick!
Now try to beg
  And do a trick.
    Little pup,
      Sit up!

Say! little pup,
    Chime up!
Why, you can sing--
  Now come with me;
Let's wash and eat

And then we'll see,
  Little pup,
    What's up!

-HENRY FIRTH WOOD.

A LAUGH IN CHURCH

She sat on the sliding cushion,
The dear, wee woman of four;
Her feet, in their shiny slippers,
Hung dangling over the floor.
She meant to be good; she had promised,
And so with her big, brown eyes,
She stared at the meetinghouse windows
And counted the crawling flies.

She looked far up at the preacher,
But she thought of the honeybees
Droning away at the blossoms
That whitened the cherry trees.
She thought of a broken basket,
Where curled in a dusky heap,
Four sleek, round puppies, with fringy ears.
Lay snuggled and fast asleep.

Such soft, warm bodies to cuddle,

Such queer little hearts to beat,
Such swift round tongues to kiss,
Such sprawling, cushiony feet;
She could feel in her clasping fingers
The touch of the satiny skin,
And a cold, wet nose exploring
The dimples under her chin.

Then a sudden ripple of laughter
Ran over the parted lips
So quick that she could not catch it
With her rosy finger-tips.
The people whispered "Bless the child,"
As each one waked from a nap,
But the dear, wee woman hid her face
For shame in her mother's lap.

   -ANONYMOUS.

TREASURES

They got a bran' new baby
  At Bud Hicks' house, you see.
You'd think Bud Hicks had somethin'
  The way he talks to me!
He comes around a-braggin',
  An' when he wouldn't quit

The Human Relationship

I said: "What good's a baby?
  You can't hunt fleas on it."

Then Bud turned to me an' told me
  How loud that kid could yell,
An' lots I can't remember,
  He had so much to tell.
But I got tired o' hearin'
  An' so I ast him, quick,
"If you wuz in a-swimmin'
  Could it go get a stick?"

There is no use a-talkin',
  Bud thinks their baby's fine!
Huh! I'd a whole lot rather
  Jest have a pup like mine.
I'll bet it's not bald-headed!
  But if Bud doesn't fail
To let me hear it yellin',
  I'll let him pull Spot's tail.

  -ANONYMOUS.

THAT THERE LONG DOG

Funniest little feller
You'd ever want to see!

Browner 'an the brownest leaf
In the autumn tree.
Shortest little bow legs!
Jes' barely touch the floor--
And long--b'gosh, the longest dog
I ever seen afore!

But he's mighty amusin',
For all 'at he's so queer,
Eyes so mighty solemn,
Askin' like an' clear,
And when he puts his paws up,
Head stuck on one side--
Jes' naturally love every hair
In his durn Dutch hide.

   -ALICE GILL FERGUSON.

MY FRIEND

True and trustful, never doubting,
Is my young and handsome friend;
     Always jolly,
     Full of fun,
     Bright eyes gleaming
     Like the sun--
Never see him blue or pouting

The Human Relationship

From the day's break to its end.

Whether I am "flush" or "busted"
Makes no difference to him!
    "Let's be gay, sir"--
    He would say, sir--
    "Won't have any
    Other way, sir!"
Oh, he's never cross and crusted--
Light of heart and full of vim!

Often we go out together
For a ramble far and wide--
    Catch the breezes
    Fresh and strong
    Down the mountain
    Swept along--
For we never mind the weather
When we two are side by side.

But my friend is sometimes quiet,
And I've caught his clear brown eye
    Gazing at me,
    Mute, appealing--
    Telling something,
    Yet concealing,
Yes, he'd like to talk! Well, try it--
"Bow, wow, wow," and that's his cry!

  -ANONYMOUS.

TED

I have a little brindle dog,
Seal-brown from tail to head.
His name I guess is Theodore,
But I just call him Ted.

He's only eight months old to-day
I guess he's just a pup;
Pa says he won't be larger
When he is all grown up.

He plays around about the house,
As good as he can be,
He don't seem like a little dog,
He's just like folks to me.

And when it is my bed-time,
Ma opens up the bed;
Then I nestle down real cozy
And just make room for Ted

And oh, how nice we cuddle!
He doesn't fuss or bite,
Just nestles closely up to me
And lays there still all night.

We love each other dearly,
My little Ted and me.
We're just good chums together,

The Human Relationship

And always hope to be.

-MAXINE ANNA BUCK.

LITTLE LOST PUP

He was lost!--Not a shade of doubt of that;
For he never barked at a slinking cat,
But stood in the square where the wind blew raw,
With a drooping ear, and a trembling paw,
And a mournful look in his pleading eye,
And a plaintive sniff at the passer-by
That begged as plain as a tongue could sue,
"Oh, Mister, please may I follow you?"
A lorn, wee waif of a tawny brown
Adrift in the roar of a heedless town.
Oh, the saddest of sights in a world of sin
Is a little lost pup with his tail tucked in!

Well, he won my heart (for I set great store
On my own red Bute, who is here no more)
So I whistled clear, and he trotted up,
And who so glad as that small lost pup?

Now he shares my board, and he owns my bed,
And he fairly shouts when he hears my tread.
Then if things go wrong, as they sometimes do,

And the world is cold, and I'm feeling blue,
He asserts his right to assuage my woes
With a warm, red tongue and a nice, cold nose,
And a silky head on my arm or knee,
And a paw as soft as a paw can be.

When we rove the woods for a league about
He's as full of pranks as a school let out;
For he romps and frisks like a three-months colt,
And he runs me down like a thunder-bolt.
Oh, the blithest of sights in the world so fair
Is a gay little pup with his tail in air!

　-ANONYMOUS.

MY BRINDLE BULL-TERRIER

My brindle bull-terrier, loving and wise,
With his little screw-tail and his wonderful eyes,
With his white little breast and his white little paws
Which, alas! he mistakes very often for claws;
With his sad little gait as he comes from the fight
When he feels that he hasn't done all that he might;
Oh, so fearless of man, yet afraid of a frog,
My near little, queer little, dear little dog!

He shivers and shivers and shakes with the cold;

The Human Relationship

He huddles and cuddles, though three summers old.
And forsaking the sunshine, endeavors to rove
With his cold little worriments under the stove!

At table, his majesty, dying for meat,--
Yet never despising a lump that is sweet,--
Sits close by my side with his head on my knee
And steals every good resolution from me!
How can I withhold from those worshipping eyes
A small bit of something that stealthily flies
Down under the table and into his mouth
As I tell my dear neighbor of life in the South.

My near little, queer little, dear little dog,
So fearless of man, yet afraid of a frog!
The nearest and queerest and dearest of all
The race that is loving and winning and small;
The sweetest, most faithful, the truest and best
Dispenser of merriment, love and unrest!

   -COLETTA RYAN.

LAUTH

He was a gash and faithfu' tyke
As ever lapt a sheugh or dyke.
His honest, sawnsie, bawsint face

Aye gat him friends in ilka place.
His breast was white, his towsie back
Weel clad wi' coat o' glossy black.
His gawcie tail, wi' upward curl,
Hung ower his hurdies wi' a swurl.

 -ROBERT BURNS.

THE DROWNED SPANIEL

  The day-long bluster of the storm was o'er,
The sands were bright; the winds had fallen asleep,
And, from the far horizon, o'er the deep
  The sunset swam unshadowed to the shore.

  High up, the rainbow had not passed away,
When, roving o'er the shingle beach, I found
A little waif, a spaniel newly drowned;
  The shining waters kissed him as he lay.

In some kind heart thy gentle memory dwells,
I said, and, though thy latest aspect tells
  Of drowning pains and mortal agony,
  Thy master's self might weep and smile to see
His little dog stretched on these rosy shells,
  Betwixt the rainbow and the rosy sea.

 -CHARLES TENNYSON TURNER.

The Human Relationship

2

The Human Relationship

A man's dog stands by him in prosperity and in poverty, in health and in sickness. He will sleep on the cold ground, where the wintry winds blow and the snow drives fiercely, if only he can be near his master's side. He will kiss the hand that has no food to offer, he will lick the wounds and sores that come in encounter with the roughness of the world. When all other friends desert, he remains. When riches take wings, and reputation falls to pieces, he is as constant in his love as the sun in its journey through the heavens.

The Human Relationship

CLUNY

I am quite sure he thinks that I am God--
Since he is God on whom each one depends
For life, and all things that his bounty sends--
My dear old dog, most constant of all friends;

Not quick to mind, but quicker far than I
To him whom God I know and own; his eye,
Deep brown and liquid, watches for my nod;
He is more patient underneath the rod

Than I, when God his wise corrections sends.
He looks love at me deep as words e'er spake,
And from me never crumb or sup will take
But he wags thanks with his most vocal tail.

And when some crashing noise wakes all his fear
He is content and quiet if I'm near,
Secure that my protection will prevail!

So, faithful, mindful, thankful, trustful, he
Tells me what I unto my God should be.

  -WILLIAM CROSWELL DOANE.

THE BEST FRIEND

If I was sad, then he had grief, as well--
Seeking my hands with soft insistent paw,
Searching my face with anxious eyes that saw
More than my halting, human speech could tell;
Eyes wide with wisdom, fine, compassionate--
Dear, loyal one, that knew not wrong nor hate.

If I made merry--then how he would strive
To show his joy; "Good master, let's to play,
The world is ours," that gladsome bark would say;
"Just yours and mine--'tis fun to be alive!"
Our world ... four walls above the city's din,
My crutch the bar that ever held us in.

Whate'er my mood--the fretful word, or sweet,
The swift command, the wheedling undertone,
His faith was fixed, his love was mine, alone,
His heaven was here at my slow crippled feet:
Oh, friend thrice-lost; oh, fond heart unassailed,
Ye taught me trust when man's dull logic failed.

-MERIBAH ABBOTT.

The Human Relationship

MY DOG AND I

When living seems but little worth
And all things go awry,
I close the door, we journey forth--
My dog and I!

For books and pen we leave behind,
But little careth he,
His one great joy in life is just
To be with me.

He notes by just one upward glance
My mental attitude,
As on we go past laughing stream
And singing wood.

The soft winds have a magic touch
That brings to care release,
The trees are vocal with delight,
The rivers sing of peace.

How good it is to be alive!
Nature, the healer strong,
Has set each pulse with life athrill
And joy and song.

Discouragement! 'Twas but a name,
And all things that annoy,
Out in the lovely world of June

Life seemeth only joy!

And ere we reach the busy town,
Like birds my troubles fly,
We are two comrades glad of heart--
My dog and I!

  -ALICE J. CLEATOR.

MY GENTLEMAN

I own a dog who is a gentleman;
By birth most surely, since the creature can
Boast of a pedigree the like of which
Holds not a Howard nor a Metternich.

By breeding. Since the walks of life he trod
He never wagged an unkind tale abroad,
He never snubbed a nameless cur because
Without a friend or credit card he was.

By pride. He looks you squarely in the face
Unshrinking and without a single trace
Of either diffidence or arrogant
Assertion such as upstarts often flaunt.

By tenderness. The littlest girl may tear

The Human Relationship

With absolute impunity his hair,
And pinch his silken, flowing ears, the while
He smiles upon her--yes, I've seen him smile.

By loyalty. No truer friend than he
Has come to prove his friendship's worth to me.
He does not fear the master--knows no fear--
But loves the man who is his master here.

By countenance. If there be nobler eyes,
More full of honor and of honesties,
In finer head, on broader shoulders found,
Then have I never met the man or hound.

Here is the motto on my lifeboat's log:
"God grant I may be worthy of my dog!"

 -ANONYMOUS.

THE DEAD BOY'S PORTRAIT AND HIS DOG

Day after day I have come and sat
Beseechingly upon the mat,
Wistfully wondering where you are at.

Why have they placed you on the wall,

Dog Poems

So deathly still, so strangely tall?
You do not turn from me, nor call.

Why do I never hear my name?
Why are you fastened in a frame?
You are the same, and not the same.

Away from me why do you stare
So far out in the distance where
I am not? I am here! Not there!

What has your little doggie done?
You used to whistle me to run
Beside you, or ahead, for fun!

You used to pat me, and a glow
Of pleasure through my life would go!
How is it that I shiver so?

My tail was once a waving flag
Of welcome. Now I cannot wag
It for the weight I have to drag.

I know not what has come to me.
'Tis only in my sleep I see
Things smiling as they used to be.

I do not dare to bark; I plead
But dumbly, and you never heed;
Nor my protection seem to need.

The Human Relationship

I watch the door, I watch the gate;
I am watching early, watching late,
Your doggie still!--I watch and wait.

　-GERALD MASSEY.

ADVICE TO A DOG PAINTER

Happiest of the spaniel race,
Painter, with thy colors grace,
Draw his forehead large and high,
Draw his blue and humid eye;
Draw his neck, so smooth and round,
Little neck with ribands bound;
And the musely swelling breast
Where the Loves and Graces rest;
And the spreading, even back,
Soft, and sleek, and glossy black;
And the tail that gently twines,
Like the tendrils of the vines;
And the silky twisted hair,
Shadowing thick the velvet ear;
Velvet ears which, hanging low,
O'er the veiny temples flow.

　-JONATHAN SWIFT.

Dog Poems

MERCY'S REWARD

      Hast seen
The record written of Salah-ud-Deen,
The Sultan--how he met, upon a day,
In his own city on the public way,
A woman whom they led to die? The veil
Was stripped from off her weeping face, and pale
Her shamed cheeks were, and wild her fixed eye,
And her lips drawn with terror at the cry
Of the harsh people, and the rugged stones
Borne in their hands to break her flesh and bones;
For the law stood that sinners such as she
Perish by stoning, and this doom must be;
So went the adult'ress to her death.
High noon it was, and the hot Khamseen's breath
Blew from the desert sands and parched the town.
The crows gasped, and the kine went up and down
With lolling tongues; the camels moaned; a crowd
Pressed with their pitchers, wrangling high and loud
About the tank; and one dog by a well,
Nigh dead with thirst, lay where he yelped and fell,
Glaring upon the water out of reach,
And praying succour in a silent speech,
So piteous were its eyes.
             Which, when she saw,
This woman from her foot her shoe did draw,
Albeit death-sorrowful, and, looping up
The long silk of her girdle, made a cup
Of the heel's hollow, and thus let it sink

The Human Relationship

Until it touched the cool black water's brink;
So filled th' embroidered shoe, and gave a draught
To the spent beast, which whined, and fawned, and quaffed
Her kind gift to the dregs; next licked her hand,
With such glad looks that all might understand
He held his life from her; then, at her feet
He followed close, all down the cruel street,
Her one friend in that city.
        But the King,
Riding within his litter, marked this thing,
And how the woman, on her way to die
Had such compassion for the misery
Of that parched hound: "Take off her chain, and place
The veil once more about the sinner's face,
And lead her to her house in peace!" he said.
"The law is that the people stone thee dead
For that which thou hast wrought; but there is come
Fawning around thy feet a witness dumb,
Not heard upon thy trial; this brute beast
Testifies for thee, sister! whose weak breast
Death could not make ungentle. I hold rule
In Allah's stead, who is 'the Merciful,'
And hope for mercy; therefore go thou free--
I dare not show less pity unto thee."

As we forgive--and more than we--
Ya Barr! Good God, show clemency.

-SIR EDWIN ARNOLD.

BEAU AND THE WATER LILY

The noon was shady, and soft airs
  Swept Ouse's silent tide,
When 'scaped from literary cares
  I wandered on his side.

My spaniel, prettiest of his race,
  And high in pedigree
(Two nymphs adorned with every grace
  That spaniel found for me)

Now wantoned, lost in flags and reeds,
  Now starting into sight,
Pursued the swallow o'er the meads
  With scarce a slower flight.

It was the time that Ouse displayed
  His lilies newly blown;
Their beauties I intent surveyed,
  And one I wished my own.

With cane extended far I sought
  To steer it close to land;
But still the prize, though nearly caught,
  Escaped my eager hand.

Beau marked my unsuccessful pains
  With fixed, considerate face,
And puzzling, set his puppy brains

The Human Relationship

  To comprehend the case.

But with a chirrup clear and strong
  Dispersing all his dream,
I thence withdrew, and followed long
  The windings of the stream.

My ramble ended, I returned;
  Beau trotting far before
The floating wreath again discerned,
  And, plunging, left the shore.

I saw him, with that lily cropped,
  Impatient swim to meet
My quick approach, and soon he dropped
  The treasure at my feet.

Charmed with the sight, "The world," I cried,
  "Shall hear of this thy deed;
My dog shall mortify the pride
  Of man's superior breed:

"But chief myself I will enjoin
  Awake at duty's call,
To show a love as prompt as thine
  To Him who gives me all."

  -WILLIAM COWPER.

Dog Poems

PETRONIUS

A dog there was, Petronius by name--
A cur of no degree, yet which the same
Rejoiced him; because so worthless he
That in his worthlessness remarkably
He shone, th' example de luxe of how a cur
May be the very limit of a slur
Upon the honored name of dog; a joke
He was, a satire blasphemous; he broke
The records all for sheer insulting "bunk;"
No dog had ever breathed who was so punk!

And yet that cur, Petronius by name,
Enkindled in his master's heart a flame
Of love, affection, reverence, so rare
That had he been an angel bright and fair
The homage paid him had been less; you see
The red-haired boy who owned him had a bee--
There was no other dog on land or sea.
Petronius was solid; he just was
The dog, the only dog on earth, because--
Because a red-haired boy who likes his dog,
He likes that dog so much no other dog
Exists--and that, my friends, is loyalty,
Than which there is no grander ecstasy.

  -FREDERIC P. LADD.

The Human Relationship

MY DOG

Here is a friend who proves his worth
Without conceit or pride of birth.
Let want or plenty play the host,
He gets the least and gives the most--
     He's just a dog.

He's ever faithful, kind and true;
He never questions what I do,
And whether I may go or stay,
He's always ready to obey
     'Cause he's a dog.

Such meager fare his want supplies!
A hand caress, and from his eyes
There beams more love than mortals know;
Meanwhile he wags his tail to show
     That he's my dog.

He watches me all through the day,
And nothing coaxes him away;
And through the night-long slumber deep
He guards the home wherein I sleep--
     And he's a dog.

I wonder if I'd be content
To follow where my master went,
And where he rode--as needs he must--
Would I run after in his dust

Dog Poems

    Like other dogs.

How strange if things were quite reversed--
The man debased, the dog put first.
I often wonder how 'twould be
Were he the master 'stead of me--
    And I the dog.

A world of deep devotion lies
Behind the windows of his eyes;
Yet love is only half his charm--
He'd die to shield my life from harm.
    Yet he's a dog.

If dogs were fashioned out of men
What breed of dog would I have been?
And would I e'er deserve caress,
Or be extolled for faithfulness
    Like my dog here?

As mortals go, how few possess
Of courage, trust, and faithfulness
Enough from which to undertake,
Without some borrowed traits, to make
    A decent dog!

-JOSEPH M. ANDERSON.

CHARITY'S EYE

One evening Jesus lingered in the marketplace,
Teaching the people parables of truth and grace,
When in the square remote a crowd was seen to rise,
And stop with loathing gestures and abhorring cries.
The Master and his meek disciples went to see
What cause for this commotion and disgust could be,
And found a poor dead dog beside the gutter laid--
Revolting sight! at which each face its hate betrayed.

One held his nose, one shut his eyes, one turned away,
And all among themselves began to say:
"Detested creature! he pollutes the earth and air!"
"His eyes are blear!" "His ears are foul!" "His ribs are bare!"
"In his torn hide there's not a decent shoestring left,
No doubt the execrable cur was hung for theft."
Then Jesus spake, and dropped on him the saving wreath:
"Even pearls are dark before the whiteness of his teeth."

The pelting crowd grew silent and ashamed, like one
Rebuked by sight of wisdom higher than his own;
And one exclaimed: "No creature so accursed can be
But some good thing in him a loving eye will see."

-WILLIAM ROUNSEVILLE ALGER.

TO BLANCO

My dear, dumb friend, low-lying there,
  A willing vassal at my feet,
Glad partner of my home and fare,
  My shadow in the street,

I look into your great, brown eyes,
  Where love and loyal homage shine,
And wonder where the difference lies
  Between your soul and mine.

For all of good that I have found
  Within myself, or human kind,
Hath royally informed and crowned
  Your gentle heart and mind.

I scan the whole broad earth around
  For that one heart which, leal and true,
Bears friendship without end or bound,
  And find the prize in you.

I trust you as I trust the stars;
  Nor cruel loss, nor scoff, nor pride,
Nor beggary, nor dungeon bars,
  Can move you from my side.

As patient under injury
  As any Christian saint of old,
As gentle as a lamb with me,

But with your brothers bold.

More playful than a frolic boy,
  More watchful than a sentinel,
By day and night your constant joy
  To guard and please me well.

I clasp your head upon my breast,
  The while you whine, and lick my hand;
And thus our friendship is confessed,
  And thus we understand.

Ah, Blanco! Did I worship God
  As truly as you worship me,
Or follow where my Master trod
  With your humility,

Did I sit fondly at His feet,
  As you, dear Blanco, sit at mine,
And watch Him with a love as sweet,
  My life would grow divine.

  -J.G. HOLLAND.

THE OULD HOUND

When Shamus made shift wid a turf-hut

Dog Poems

He'd naught but a hound to his name;
And whither he went thrailed the ould friend,
  Dog-faithful and iver the same!

And he'd gnaw thro' a rope in the night-time,
  He'd eat thro' a wall or a door,
He'd shwim thro' a lough in the winther,
  To be wid his master wanst more!

And the two, faith, would share their last bannock;
  They'd share their last collop and bone;
And deep in the starin' ould sad eyes
  Lean Shamus would stare wid his own!

And loose hung the flanks av the ould hound
  When Shamus lay sick on his bed--
Ay, waitin' and watchin' wid sad eyes
  He'd eat not av bone or av bread!

But Shamus be springtime grew betther,
  And a trouble came into his mind;
And he'd take himself off to the village,
  And be leavin' his hound behind!

And deep was the whine of the ould dog
  Wid a love that was deeper than life--
But be Michaelmas, faith, it was whispered
  That Shamus was takin' a wife!

A wife and a fine house he got him;
  In a shay he went drivin' around;

The Human Relationship

And I met him be chance at the cross-roads,
  And I says to him, "How's the ould hound?"

"My wife never took to that ould dog,"
  Says he, wid a shrug av his slats,
"So we've got us a new dog from Galway,
  And och, he's the divil for rats!"

-ARTHUR STRINGER.

THE MISER'S ONLY FRIEND

There watched a cur before the miser's gate--
A very cur, whom all men seemed to hate;
Gaunt, shaggy, savage, with an eye that shone
Like a live coal; and he possessed but one.
His bark was wild and eager, and became
That meager body and that eye of flame;
His master prized him much, and Fang his name,
His master fed him largely, but not that
Nor aught of kindness made the snarler fat.
Flesh he devoured, but not a bit would stay--
He barked, and snarled, and growled it all away.
His ribs were seen extended like a rack,
And coarse red hair hung roughly o'er his back.
Lamed in one leg, and bruised in wars of yore,
Now his sore body made his temper sore.

Dog Poems

Such was the friend of him who could not find,
Nor make him one, 'mong creatures of his kind.
Brave deeds of Fang his master often told,
The son of Fury, famed in deeds of old,
From Snatch and Rabid sprung; and noted they
In earlier times--each dog will have his day.

The notes of Fang were to his master known
And dear--they bore some likeness to his own;
For both conveyed, to the experienced ear,
"I snarl and bite because I hate and fear."
None passed ungreeted by the master's door,
Fang railed at all, but chiefly at the poor;
And when the nights were stormy, cold and dark,
The act of Fang was a perpetual bark.
But though the master loved the growl of Fang
There were who vowed the ugly cur to hang,
Whose angry master, watchful for his friend,
As strongly vowed his servant to defend.

In one dark night, and such as Fang before
Was ever known its tempests to outroar,
To his protector's wonder now expressed,
No angry notes--his anger was at rest.
The wond'ring master sought the silent yard,
Left Phoebe sleeping, and his door unbarred,
Nor more returned to that forsaken bed--
But lo! the morning came, and he was dead.
Fang and his master side by side were laid
In grim repose--their debt to nature paid.
The master's hand upon the cur's cold chest

The Human Relationship

Was now reclined, and had before been pressed,
As if he sought how deep and wide the wound
That laid such spirit in a sleep so sound;
And when he found it was the sleep of death
A sympathizing sorrow stopped his breath.
Close to his trusty servant he was found,
As cold his body, and his sleep as sound.

  -GEORGE CRABBE.

POOR DOG TRAY

On the green banks of Shannon, when Sheelah was nigh,
No blithe Irish lad was as happy as I;
No harp like my own could so cheerily play,
And wherever I went was my poor dog Tray.

When at last I was forced from my Sheelah to part,
She said (while the sorrow was big at her heart)
"Oh, remember your Sheelah when far, far away,
And be kind, my dear Pat, to our poor dog Tray."

Poor dog! he was faithful and kind, to be sure,
And he constantly loved me, although I was poor;
When the sour-looking folks sent me heartless away,
I had always a friend in my poor dog Tray.

Dog Poems

When the road was so dark, and the night was so cold,
And Pat and his dog were grown weary and old,
How snugly we slept in my old coat of gray,
And he licked me for kindness--my poor dog Tray.

Though my wallet was scant, I remembered his case,
Nor refused my last crust to his pitiful face;
But he died at my feet on a cold winter's day,
And I played a lament for my poor dog Tray.

Where now shall I go, poor, forsaken and blind?
Can I find one to guide me so faithful and kind?
To my sweet native village, so far, far away,
I can ne'er more return with my poor dog Tray.

   -THOMAS CAMPBELL.

MY COMFORTER

The world had all gone wrong that day
  And tired and in despair,
Discouraged with the ways of life,
  I sank into my chair.

A soft caress fell on my cheek,
  My hands were thrust apart.
And two big sympathizing eyes

Gazed down into my heart.

I had a friend; what cared I now
  For fifty worlds? I knew
One heart was anxious when I grieved--
  My dog's heart, loyal, true.

"God bless him," breathed I soft and low,
  And hugged him close and tight.
One lingering lick upon my ear
  And we were happy--quite.

-ANONYMOUS.

THE LITTLE WHITE DOG

Little white dog with the meek brown eyes,
Tell me the boon that most you prize.
Would a juicy bone meet your heart's desire?
Or a cozy rug by a blazing fire?
Or a sudden race with a truant cat?
Or a gentle word? Or a friendly pat?
Is the worn-out ball you have always near
The dearest of all the things held dear?
Or is the home you left behind
The dream of bliss to your doggish mind?
But the little white dog just shook his head

As if "None of these are best," he said.

A boy's clear whistle came from the street;
There's a wag of the tail and a twinkle of feet,
And the little white dog did not even say,
"Excuse me, ma'am," as he scampered away;
But I'm sure as can be his greatest joy
Is just to trot behind that boy.

   -MAY ELLIS NICHOLS.

THE IRISH GREYHOUND

Behold this creature's form and state;
Which nature therefore did create,
That to the world might be exprest
What mien there can be in a beast;
And that we in this shape may find
A lion of another kind.
For this heroic beast does seem
In majesty to rival him,
And yet vouchsafes to man to show
Both service and submission, too.
From whence we this distinction have,
That beast is fierce, but this is brave.
This dog hath so himself subdued
That hunger cannot make him rude,

The Human Relationship

And his behavior does confess
True courage dwells with gentleness.
With sternest wolves he dares engage,
And acts on them successful rage.
Yet too much courtesy may chance
To put him out of countenance.
When in his opposer's blood
Fortune hath made his virtue good,
This creature from an act so brave
Grows not more sullen, but more brave.
Man's guard he would be, not his sport,
Believing he hath ventured for't;
But yet no blood, or shed or spent,
Can ever make him insolent.
  Few men of him to do great things have learned,
  And when they're done to be so unconcerned.

-KATHERINE PHILLIPS.

THE VAGABONDS

We are two travellers, Roger and I.
Roger's my dog.--Come here, you scamp!
Jump for the gentleman,--mind your eye!
Over the table,--look out for the lamp!
The rogue is growing a little old;
Five years we've tramped through wind and weather,

Dog Poems

And slept out-doors when nights were cold,
And ate and drank--and starved--together.

We've learned what comfort is, I tell you!
A bed on the floor, a bit of rosin,
A fire to thaw our thumbs (poor fellow!
The paw he holds up there's been frozen),
Plenty of catgut for my fiddle
(This out-door business is bad for strings),
Then a few nice buckwheats hot from the griddle,
And Roger and I set up for kings!

No, thank ye, Sir,--I never drink;
Roger and I are exceedingly moral,--
Aren't we, Roger?--See him wink!--
Well, something hot, then,--we won't quarrel.
He's thirsty, too,--see him nod his head?
What a pity, Sir, that dogs can't talk!
He understands every word that's said,--
And he knows good milk from water-and-chalk.

The truth is, Sir, now I reflect,
I've been so sadly given to grog,
I wonder I've not lost the respect
(Here's to you, Sir!) even of my dog.
But he sticks by, through thick and thin;
And this old coat with its empty pockets,
And rags that smell of tobacco and gin,
He'll follow while he has eyes in his sockets.

There isn't another creature living

The Human Relationship

Would do it, and prove, through every disaster,
So fond, so faithful, and so forgiving,
To such a miserable, thankless master!
No, Sir!--see him wag his tail and grin!
By George! it makes my old eyes water!
That is, there's something in this gin
That chokes a fellow. But no matter!

We'll have some music, if you're willing,
And Roger (hem! what a plague a cough is, Sir!)
Shall march a little--Start, you villain!
Paws up! Eyes front! Salute your officer!
'Bout face! Attention! Take your rifle!
(Some dogs have arms, you see!) Now hold your
Cap while the gentlemen give a trifle,
To aid a poor old patriot soldier!

March! Halt! Now show how the rebel shakes
When he stands up to hear his sentence.
Now tell us how many drams it takes
To honor a jolly new acquaintance.
Five yelps,--that's five; he's mighty knowing!
The night's before us, fill the glasses!--
Quick, Sir! I'm ill,--my brain is going!--
Some brandy,--thank you,--there!--it passes!

Why not reform? That's easily said;
But I've gone through such wretched treatment,
Sometimes forgetting the taste of bread,
And scarce remembering what meat meant,
That my poor stomach's past reform;

And there are times when, mad with thinking,
I'd sell out heaven for something warm
To prop a horrible inward sinking.

Is there a way to forget to think?
At your age, Sir, home, fortune, friends,
A dear girl's love,--but I took to drink,--
The same old story; you know how it ends.
If you could have seen these classic features,--
You needn't laugh, Sir; they were not then
Such a burning libel on God's creatures:
I was one of your handsome men!

If you had seen _her_, so fair and young,
Whose head was happy on this breast!
If you could have heard the songs I sung
When the wine went round, you wouldn't have guessed
That ever I, Sir, should be straying
From door to door, with fiddle and dog,
Ragged and penniless, and playing
To you to-night for a glass of grog!

She's married since,--a parson's wife:
'Twas better for her that we should part,--
Better the soberest, prosiest life
Than a blasted home and a broken heart.
I have seen her? Once: I was weak and spent
On the dusty road: a carriage stopped:
But little she dreamed, as on she went,
Who kissed the coin that her fingers dropped!

The Human Relationship

You've set me talking, Sir; I'm sorry:
It makes me wild to think of the change!
What do you care for a beggar's story?
Is it amusing? You find it strange?
I had a mother so proud of me!
'Twas well she died before.--Do you know
If the happy spirits in heaven can see
The ruin and wretchedness here below?

Another glass, and strong, to deaden
This pain; then Roger and I will start.
I wonder, has he such a lumpish, leaden,
Aching thing in place of a heart?
He is sad sometimes, and would weep, if he could,
No doubt remembering things that were,--
A virtuous kennel, with plenty of food,
And himself a sober, respectable cur.

I'm better now; that glass was warming.--
You rascal! limber your lazy feet!
We must be fiddling and performing
For supper and bed, or starve in the street.--
Not a very gay life to lead, you think?
But soon we shall go where lodgings are free,
And the sleepers need neither victuals nor drink:--
The sooner, the better for Roger and me!

-J.T. TROWBRIDGE.

IN CINEAM

Thou dogged Cineas, hated like a dog,
For still thou grumblest like a masty dog,
Compar'st thyself to nothing but a dog;
Thou say'st thou art as weary as a dog,
As angry, sick, and hungry as a dog,
As dull and melancholy as a dog,
As lazy, sleepy, idle as a dog.
But why dost thou compare thee to a dog
In that for which all men despise a dog?
I will compare thee better to a dog;
Thou art as fair and comely as a dog,
Thou art as true and honest as a dog,
Thou art as kind and liberal as a dog,
Thou art as wise and valiant as a dog,
But, Cineas, I have often heard thee tell
Thou art as like thy father as may be:
'Tis like enough; and, faith, I like it well;
But I am glad thou art not like to me.

  -SIR JOHN DAVIES.

OLD MATTHEW'S DOG

I am only a dog, and I've had my day;

The Human Relationship

So, idle and dreaming, stretched out I lay
In the welcome warmth of the summer sun,
  A poor old hunter whose work is done.

Dream? Yes, indeed; though I am but a dog.
  Don't I dream of the partridge I sprung by the log?
Of the quivering hare and her desperate flight,
  Of the nimble gray squirrel secure in his height,

Far away in the top of the hickory tree,
  Looking down safe and saucy at Matthew and me,
Till the hand, true and steady, a messenger shot,
  And the creature upbounded, and fell, and was not?

Old Matthew was king of the wood-rangers then;
  And the quails in the stubble, the ducks in the fen,
The hare on the common, the birds on the bough,
  Were afraid. They are safe enough now,

For all we can harm them, old master and I.
  We have had our last hunt, the game must go by,
While Matthew sits fashioning bows in the door,
  For a living. We'll never hunt more.

For time, cold and hardship have stiffened his knee,
  And since little Lottie died, often I see
His hands tremble sorely, and go to his eyes,
  For the lost baby daughter, so pretty and wise.

Oh, it's sad to be old, and to see the blue sky
  Look far away to the dim, fading eye;

Dog Poems

To feel the fleet foot growing weary and sore
  That in forest and hamlet shall lag evermore.

I am going--I hear the great wolf on my track;
  Already around me his shadow falls black.
One hunting cry more! Oh, master, come nigh,
  And lay the white paw in your own as I die!

Oh, come to me, master; the last hedge is passed--
  Our tramps in the wildwood are over at last;
Stoop lower, and lay my head on your knee.
  What! Tears for a useless old hunter like me?

You will see little Lottie again by and by.
  I shan't. They don't have any dogs in the sky.
Tell her, loving and trusty, beside you I died,
  And--bury me, master, not far from her side.

For we loved little Lottie so well, you and I.
  Ha, master, the shadow! Fire low--it is nigh--
There was never a sound in the still morning heard,
  But the heart of the hunter his old jacket stirred.

As he flung himself down on the brute's shaggy coat,
  And watched the faint life in its quivering throat
Till it stopped quite at last. The black wolf had won,
  And the death-hunted hound into cover had run.

But long ere the snow over graves softly fell,
  Old Matthew was resting from labor as well;
While the cottage stood empty, yet back from the hill

The voice of the hound in the morn echoed still.

-ANONYMOUS.

A DOG AND A MAN

He was a dog,
    But he stayed at home
    And guarded the family night and day.
He was a dog
    That didn't roam.
    He lay on the porch or chased the stray--
    The tramps, the burglar, the hen, away;
    For a dog's true heart for that household beat
    At morning and evening, in cold and heat.
He was a dog.

He was a man,
    And didn't stay
    To cherish his wife and his children fair.
He was a man.
    And every day
    His heart grew callous, its love-beats rare,
    He thought of himself at the close of day,
    And, cigar in his fingers, hurried away
    To the club, the lodge, the store, the show.
    But--he had a right to go, you know.

He was a man.

-ANONYMOUS.

ROVER-DOG

Old Rover-Dog, he toasts his toes
  Right by th' chimney-fire wif me.
I turned his long ear wrong side out
  An' he was s'rprised as he could be!
An' nen he reached right out an' took
  An' int'rest in my lolly-pop--
That's w'y I shook my finger hard
  At him, 'cause he jus' better stop.

I ast him which his sweet toof was,
  An' he jus' laffed an' showed me where
He keeps um, up an' down his mouf--
  (I guess there's mos' a hundred there).
He's got a cunning little house,
  But you can't climb right in, at all--
Ain't hardly big enough for him;
  I guess it is a size too small.

'Cause when he is "at home" his head
  Stays looking out of his front door;
His paws hang out convenient like,

The Human Relationship

So's folks they will shake hands some more.
Old Rover-Dog, w'en he likes folks,
  He thumps th' floor hard wif his tail--
Where 'tis you've heard that sound before
  Is w'en your pa, he drives a nail.

One time my Uncle Fred p'tend
  He's "tramp-mans" an' will come right in;
I put my ear on Rover's back
  So's I could hear th' growl begin.
An' oncet he thought he'd try his nap
  Right in my grampa's big armchair.
My grampa, he sat down on him,
  'Cause "he wa'n't 'spectin' dogs was there."

'N Rover walked off dignified
  An' curled his back up 'gainst th' wall--
If grampas ain't got manners, w'y,
  He isn't goin' to care at all.
That's w'y I went an' 'xplained to him
  How grampas, they ain't imperlite,
A grampa has th' bestest chair
  Because his hair is very white.

Nen Rover-Dog raise up one ear
  An' lift his nose fum off his paw,
An' say his feelin's aren't all hurt
  If that was _candy_ that he saw!
'N w'en he'd et my choc'late cream
  He went an' finished up his dream.

Dog Poems

-MARIE LOUISE TOMPKINS.

HORSE, DOG AND MAN

The horse and the dog had tamed a man and
    fastened him to a fence:
Said the horse to the dog: "For the life of
    me, I don't see a bit of sense
In letting him have the thumbs that grow at
    the sides of his hands. Do you?"
And the dog looked solemn and shook his head,
    and said: "I'm a goat if I do!"

The poor man groaned and tried to get loose,
    and sadly he begged them, "Stay!
You will rob me of things for which I have
    use by cutting my thumbs away!
You will spoil my looks, you will cause me
    pain; ah, why would you treat me so?
As I am, God made me, and He knows best!
    Oh, masters, pray let me go!"

The dog laughed out, and the horse replied,
    "Oh, the cutting won't hurt you, see?
We'll have a hot iron to clap right on, as you
    did in your docking of me!
God gave you your thumbs and all, but still,

The Human Relationship

    the Creator, you know, may fail
To do the artistic thing, as he did in the
    furnishing me with a tail."

So they bound the man and cut off his thumbs,
    and were deaf to his pitiful cries,
And they seared the stumps, and they viewed
    their work through happy and dazzled eyes.
"How trim he appears," the horse exclaimed,
    "since his awkward thumbs are gone!
For the life of me I cannot see why the Lord
    ever put them on!"

"Still it seems to me," the dog replied, "that
    there's something else to do;
His ears look rather too long for me, and how
    do they look to you?"
The man cried out: "Oh, spare my ears!
    God fashioned them as you see,
And if you apply your knife to them, you'll
    surely disfigure me."

"But you didn't disfigure me, you know," the
    dog decisively said,
"When you bound me fast and trimmed my
    ears down close to the top of my head!"
So they let him moan and they let him groan
    while they cropped his ears away,
And they praised his looks when they let him
    up, and proud indeed were they.

But that was years and years ago, in an
    unenlightened age!
Such things are ended, now, you know; we've
    reached a higher stage.
The ears and thumbs God gave to man are his
    to keep and wear,
And the cruel horse and dog look on, and
    never appear to care.

  -S.E. KISER.

THE BEST DOG

 Yes, I went to see the bow-wows, and I looked at every one,
  Proud dogs of each breed and strain that's underneath the sun;
  But not one could compare with--you may hear it with surprise--
  A little yellow dog I know that never took a prize.

 Not that they would have skipped him when they gave the ribbons out,
  Had there been a class to fit him--though his lineage is in doubt.
  No judge of dogs could e'er resist the honest, faithful eyes
  Of that plain little yellow dog that never took a prize.

The Human Relationship

Suppose he wasn't trained to hunt, and never killed a rat,
And isn't much on tricks or looks or birth--well, what of that?
That might be said of lots of folks whom men call great and wise,
As well as of that yellow dog that never took a prize.

It isn't what a dog can do, or what a dog may be,
That hits a man. It's simply this--does he believe in me?
And by that test I know there's not the compeer 'neath the skies
Of that plain little yellow dog that never took a prize.

Oh, he's the finest little pup that ever wagged a tail,
And followed man with equal joy to Congress or to jail.
I'm going to start a special show--'Twill beat the world for size--
For faithful little yellow dogs, and each shall have a prize.

-ANONYMOUS.

CÆSAR, KING EDWARD'S DOG

No deeper, truer love could spring
  Spontaneously from human breast
Than Cæsar's, who has loved the king

Dog Poems

With all a dear dog's silent zest.

A dog's dumb way may not impart
 The grief that mortals can express,
But who shall say that Cæsar's heart
 Mourns his beloved king the less?

Since ours the faith, "Love lives in space,"
 His love, whene'er his soul takes wing,
May be ordained, by Heaven's grace,
 To reach the spirit of the king.

 -O. MIDDLETON.

JUST OUR DOG

He was just a dog, mister--that's all;
And all of us boys called him Bub;
He was curly and not very tall
And he hadn't a tail--just a stub.
His tail froze one cold night, you see;
We just pulled the rest of him through.
No--he didn't have much pedigree--
Perhaps that was frozen off, too.

He always seemed quite well behaved,
And he never had many bad fights;

The Human Relationship

In summer he used to be shaved
And he slept in the woodshed o' nights.
Sometimes he would wake up too soon
And cry, if his tail got a chill;
Some nights he would bark at the moon,
But some nights he would sleep very still.

He knew how to play hide-and-seek
And he always would come when you'd call;
He would play dead, roll over and speak,
And learned it in no time at all.
Sometimes he would growl, just in play,
But he never would bite, and his worst
Was to bark at the postman one day,
But the postman, he barked at him first.

He used to chase cats up a tree,
But that was just only in fun;
And a cat was as safe as could be--
Unless it should start out to run;
Sometimes he'd chase children and throw
Them down, just while running along,
And then lick their faces to show
He didn't mean anything wrong.

He was chasing an automobile
When the wheel hit him right in the side,
So he just gave a queer little squeal
And curled up and stretched out and died.
His tail it was not very long,
He was curly and not very tall;

But he never did anything wrong--
He was just our dog, mister--that's all.

  -ANONYMOUS.

RAGGED ROVER

I have still a vision of him
Ragged Rover, as he lay
In the sunshine of the morning
On the door-stone worn and gray;
Where the honeysuckle trellis
Hung its tinted blossoms low,
And the well-sweep with its bucket
Swung its burden to and fro;
Where the maples were a-quiver
In the pleasant June-time breeze;
And where droned among the phloxes
Half a hundred golden bees.

Yes, I have a vision with me
Of a home upon a hill;
And my heart is sad with longing
And my eyes with tear-drops fill.
I would be the care-free urchin
That I was so long ago
When across the sun-lit meadows

The Human Relationship

Rover with me used to go
Yonder where the graceful lindens
Threw their shadows far and cool,
And the waters waited for me
In the brimming swimming pool.

I can see him drive the cattle
From the pasture through the lane
With their mellow bells a-tinkle,
Sending out a low refrain;
I can see him drive them homeward,
Speckle, Brindle, Bess and Belle;
All the herd from down the valley
As the shades of even fell.
Thus, I wander like a pilgrim--
Slow the steps that once were strong;
Back to greet him, Ragged Rover,
And my childhood's ceaseless song.

-LESLIE CLARE MANCHESTER.

TO FLUSH, MY DOG

I

Loving friend, the gift of one
Who her own true faith has run

Dog Poems

Through thy lower nature,
Be my benediction said
With my hand upon thy head,
Gentle fellow-creature!

II

Like a lady's ringlets brown,
Flow thy silken ears adown
Either side demurely
Of thy silver-suited breast,
Shining out from all the rest
Of thy body purely.

III

Darkly brown thy body is,
Till the sunshine striking this
Alchemize its dulness,
When the sleek curls manifold
Flash all over into gold
With a burnished fulness.

IV

Underneath my stroking hand.
Startled eyes of hazel bland
Kindling, growing larger,
Up thou leanest with a spring,
Full of prank and curvetting,
Leaping like a charger.

The Human Relationship

V

Leap! thy broad tail waves a light,
Leap! thy slender feet are bright,
Canopied in fringes;
Leap! those tasselled ears of thine
Flicker strangely, fair and fine
Down their gold inches.

VI

Yet, my pretty sportive friend,
Little is't to such an end
That I praise thy rareness:
Other dogs may be thy peers
Happy in these drooping ears
And this glossy fairness.

VII

But of _thee_ it shall be said,
This dog watched beside a bed
Day and night unweary,--
Watched within a curtained room
Where no sunbeam brake the gloom,
Round the sick and dreary.

VIII

Roses, gathered for a vase,

Dog Poems

In that chamber died space,
Beam and breeze resigning:
This dog only waited on,
Knowing, that, when light is gone,
Love remains for shining.

IX

Other dogs in thymy dew
Tracked the hares, and followed through
Sunny moor or meadow:
This dog only crept and crept
Next a languid cheek that slept,
Sharing in the shadow.

X

Other dogs of loyal cheer
Bounded at the whistle clear,
Up the woodside hieing:
This dog only watched in reach
Of a faintly uttered speech,
Or a louder sighing.

XI

And if one or two quick tears
Dropped upon his glossy ears,
Or a sigh came double,
Up he sprang in eager haste,
Fawning, fondling, breathing fast,

The Human Relationship

In a tender trouble.

XII

And this dog was satisfied
If a pale, thin hand would glide
Down his dewlaps sloping,--
Which he pushed his nose within,
After,--platforming his chin
On the palm left open.

XIII

This dog, if a friendly voice
Call him now to blither choice
Than such chamber-keeping,
"Come out!" praying from the door,
Presseth backward as before,
Up against me leaping.

XIV

Therefore to this dog will I,
Tenderly, not scornfully,
Render praise and favor:
With my hand upon his head,
Is my benediction said
Therefore and forever.

XV

And because he loves me so,
Better than his kind will do
Often man or woman,
Give I back more love again
Than dogs often take of men,
Leaning from my human.

XVI

Blessings on thee, dog of mine,
Pretty collars make thee fine,
Sugared milk may fat thee!
Pleasures wag on in thy tail,
Hands of gentle motion fail
Nevermore to pat thee!

XVII

Downy pillow take thy head,
Silken coverlet bestead,
Sunshine help thy sleeping!
No fly's buzzing wake thee up,
No man break thy purple cup
Set for drinking deep in!

XVIII

Whiskered cats aroynted flee,
Sturdy stoppers keep from thee
Cologne distillations;
Nuts lie in thy path for stones,

The Human Relationship

And thy feast-day macaroons
Turn to daily rations!

XIX

Mock I thee, in wishing weal?
Tears are in my eyes to feel
Thou art made so straitly:
Blessings need must straiten too,--
Little canst thou joy or do
Thou who lovest _greatly_.

XX

Yet be blessed to the height
Of all good and all delight
Pervious to thy nature;
Only _loved_ beyond that line,
With a love that answers thine,
Loving fellow-creature!

   -ELIZABETH BARRETT BROWNING.

FRANCES

You were a friend, Frances, a friend,
With feeling and regard and capable of woe.

Dog Poems

Oh, yes, I know you were a dog, but I was just a man.
I did not buy you; no, you simply came,
Lost, and squatted on my doorstep.
The place was strange--you quivered, but stayed on,
And I had need of you.
No other fellow could make you follow him,
For you had chosen me to be your pal.
My whistle was your law,
You put your paw
Upon my palm,
And in your calm, deep eyes was writ
The promise of long comradeship.
When I came home from work,
Late and ill-tempered,
Always I heard the patter of your feet upon the oaken stairs;
Your nose was at the door-crack;
And whether I'd been bad or good that day
You fawned, and loved me just the same.
It was your way to understand.
And if I struck you, my harsh hand
Was met with your caresses.
You took my leavings, crumb and bone,
And stuck by me through thick and thin--
You were my kin.
And then one day you died
And were put deep.
But though you sleep, and ever sleep,
I sense you at my heels.

-RICHARD WIGHTMAN.

The Human Relationship

TO MY SETTER, SCOUT

You are a tried and loyal friend;
    The end
Of life will find you leal, unweary
  Of tested bonds that naught can rend,
And e'en if years be sad and dreary,
  Our plighted friendship will extend.

A truer friend man never had;
    'Tis sad
That 'mongst all earthly friends the fewest
  Unfaithful ones should thus be clad
In canine lowliness; yet truest
  They, be their treatment good or bad.

Within your eyes methinks I find
    A kind
And thoughtful look of speechless feeling
  That mem'ry's loosened cords unbind,
And let the dreamy past come stealing
  Through your dumb, reflective mind.

Scout, my trusty friend, can it be
    You see
Again, in retrospective dreaming,
  The run, the woodland, and the lea,
With past autumnal sunshine streaming
  O'er ev'ry frost-dyed field and tree?

Or do you see now once again
    The glen
And fern, the highland, and the thistle?
  And do you still remember when
We heard the bright-eyed woodcock whistle
  Down by the rippling, shrub-edged fen?

I see you turn a listening ear
    To hear
The quail upon the flower-pied heather;
  But, doggie, wait till uplands sere,
And then the autumn's waning weather
  Will bring the sport we hold so dear.

Then we will hunt the loamy swale
    And trail
The snipe, their cunning wiles o'ercoming;
  And oft will flush the bevied quail,
And hear the partridge slowly drumming
  Dull echoes in the leaf-strewn dale.

When wooded hills with crimson light
    Are bright,
We'll stroll where trees and vines are growing,
  And see birds warp their southern flight
At sundown, when the Day King's throwing
  Sly kisses to the Queen of Night.

-FRANK H. SELDEN.

The Human Relationship

WHY STRIK'ST THOU ME?

Why dost thou strike me?--Ever faithful
  In service to thee do I live;
And often when thou wert in peril
  My very utmost would I give;
  My life I would lay down for thee!
    Why strik'st thou me?

In blustering storm and cruel Winter,
  In murky night or through the day,
Obedient I have trotted by thee
  And guarded thee along the way.
  I've watched thee and protected thee:
    Why strik'st thou me?

When flashed the robber's steel against thee,
  When thou wert threatened by his arm,
And thou didst call for aid and rescue,
  Who saved thee then from mortal harm?
  My blood flowed on the sand for thee:
    Why strik'st thou me?

When down the sheer walls of the chasm
  That glooms the torrent thou didst slide,
Thou there had perished maimed and helpless
  Had I not sought thee far and wide.
  Myself forgetting, sought I thee:
    Why strik'st thou me?

When on the furious billows drifting
  Thou heldest up a beckoning hand,
And no man dared attempt to save thee,
  I brought thee safely to the land.
  From certain death I rescued thee:
    Why strik'st thou me?

Oh doom me not to starve and perish;
  The poor old Sultan do not slay!
For thee, too, will the days soon darken
  In which thy strength will fade away.
  Then thou wilt beg as I beg thee:--
    Why strik'st thou me?

-NATHAN HASKELL DOLE

CONSOLATION

Full dismal blows the wind
Without my cabin, here,
And many times I find
Myself possessed of fear.

I often hear a sound
As if a stranger tried
To enter here, but found
The door made fast inside.

The Human Relationship

The nights are filled with dread,
And fancy even scrolls
Gray visions of the dead--
Ghosts of departed souls.

But never near me creeps
What fancy oft invites.
My dog a vigil keeps
Throughout the awful nights.

  -HOWARD C. KEGLEY.

ARGUS

When wise Ulysses, from his native coast
Long kept by wars, and long by tempests tost,
Arrived at last--poor, old, despised, alone,
To all his friends, and e'en his queen, unknown,
Changed as he was, with age, and toils, and cares,
Furrowed his rev'rend face, and white his hairs,
In his own palace forced to ask his bread,
Scorned by those slaves his former bounty fed,
Forgot of all his own domestic crew,
His faithful dog his rightful master knew!

Unfed, unhoused, neglected, on the clay

Like an old servant, now cashiered, he lay;
And though ev'n then expiring on the plain,
Touched with resentment of ungrateful man,
And longing to behold his ancient lord again,
Him when he saw, he rose, and crawled to meet
('Twas all he could), and fawned, and kissed his feet,
Seized with dumb joy; then falling by his side,
Owned his returning lord, looked up, and died.

  -ALEXANDER POPE.

CHAINED IN THE YARD

'Twas only a dog in a kennel
  And little noise he made,
But it seemed to me as I heard it
  I knew what that old dog said.

"Another long month to get over;
  Will nobody loosen my chain?
Just for a run 'round the meadow,
  Then fasten me up again.

"Give me my old life of freedom,
  Give me a plunge and a swim,
A dash and a dive in the river,
  A shake and a splash on the brim."

The Human Relationship

I patted his head and spoke kindly,
 I thought that his case was hard,
Oh, give him a run in the open,
 Your dog chained up in the yard!

-ANONYMOUS.

WHY THE DOG'S NOSE IS COLD

"What makes the dog's nose always cold?"
I'll try to tell you, curls of gold,
If you will sit upon my knee
And very good and quiet be.

Well, years and years and years ago--
How many I don't really know--
There came a rain on sea and shore;
Its like was never seen before
Or since. It fell unceasing down
Till all the world began to drown.

But just before it down did pour,
An old, old man--his name was Noah--
Built him an ark, that he might save
His family from a watery grave;
And in it also he designed

To shelter two of every kind
Of beast. Well, dear, when it was done,
And heavy clouds obscured the sun,
The Noah folks to it quickly ran,
And then the animals began
To gravely march along in pairs.

The leopards, tigers, wolves and bears,
The deer, the hippopotamuses,
The rabbits, squirrels, elks, walruses,
The camels, goats, and cats, and donkeys,
The tall giraffes, the beavers, monkeys,
The rats, the big rhinoceroses,
The dromedaries and the horses,
The sheep, the mice, the kangaroos,
Hyenas, elephants, koodoos,
And many more--'twould take all day,
My dear, the very names to say--
And at the very, very end
Of the procession, by his friend
And master, faithful dog was seen.

The lifelong time he'd helping been
To drive the crowd of creatures in;
And now, with loud, exultant bark,
He gayly sprang aboard the bark.

Alas! So crowded was the space
He could not in it find a place;
So, patiently, he turned about,--
Stood half-way in, and half-way out,

The Human Relationship

And those extremely heavy showers
Descended through nine hundred hours
And more; and, darling, at their close
Most frozen was his honest nose;
And never could it lose again
The dampness of that dreadful rain.

And that is what, my curls of gold,
Made all the doggies' noses cold.

-MARGARET EYTINGE.

DOG LANGUAGE

Our Towser is the finest dog that ever wore a collar,
We wouldn't sell him--no, indeed--not even for a dollar!
I understand his language now, 'cause honest, it appears
That dogs can talk, and say a lot, with just their tails and ears.

When I come home from school he meets me with a joyous bound,
And shakes that long tail sideways, down and up, and round and round.
Pa says he's going to hang a rug beside the door to see
If Towser will not beat it while he's busy greeting me.

Then when he sees me get my hat, but thinks he cannot go,
  His ears get limp, his tail drops down, and he just walks off--slow;
  Though if I say the magic words: "Well, Towser, want to come?"
  Why, say! You'd know he answered "Yes," although at speech he's dumb.

  -MARION HOVEY BRIGGS.

A DOG'S LOYALTY

            Many a good
And useful quality, and virtue, too.
Attachment never to be weaned or changed
By any change of fortune; proof alike
Against unkindness, absence, and neglect;
Fidelity that neither bribe nor threat
Can move or warp; and gratitude for small
And trivial favors lasting as the life,
And glistening even in the dying eye.

  -ANONYMOUS.

3

The Dog In Action

Course, hunt, in hills, in valley or in plain--
   He joys to run and stretch out every limb,
To please but thee he spareth for no pain,
   His hurt (for thee) is greatest good to him.

In fields abroad he looks unto thy flocks,
   Keeping them safe from wolves and other beasts;
And oftentimes he bears away the knocks
   Of some odd thief that many a fold infests.

Dog Poems

TOLD TO THE MISSIONARY

   Just look 'ee here, Mr. Preacher, you're a-goin' a bit too fur;
   There isn't the man as is livin' as I'd let say a word agen her.
   She's a rum-lookin' bitch, that I own to, and there is a fierce look in her eyes,
   But if any cove says as she's vicious, I sez in his teeth he lies.
   Soh! Gently, old 'ooman; come here, now, and set by my side on the bed;
   I wonder who'll have yer, my beauty, when him as you're all to 's dead.
   There, stow yer palaver a minit; I knows as my end is nigh;
   Is a cove to turn round on his dog, like, just 'cos he's goin' to die?

   Oh, of course, I was sartin you'd say it. It's allus the same with you.
   Give it us straight, now, guv'nor--what would you have me do?
   Think of my soul? I do, sir. Think of my Saviour? Right!
   Don't be afeard of the bitch, sir; she's not a-goin' to bite.
   Tell me about my Saviour--tell me that tale agen,
   How he prayed for the coves as killed him, and died for the worst of men.
   It's a tale as I always liked, sir; and bound for the 'ternal shore,

The Dog In Action

I thinks it aloud to myself, sir, and I likes it more and more.

I've thumbed it out in the Bible, and I know it now by heart,
  And it's put the steam in my boiler, and made me ready to start.
  I ain't not afraid to die now; I've been a bit bad in my day,
  But I know when I knock at them portals there's one as won't say me nay.
  And it's thinkin' about that story, and all as he did for us,
  As make me so fond o' my dawg, sir; especially now I'm wus;
  For a-savin' o' folks who'd kill us is a beautiful act, the which
  I never heard tell on o' no one, 'cept o' him and o' that there bitch.

'Twas five years ago come Chrismus, maybe you remember the row,
  There was scares about hydryphoby--same as there be just now;
  And the bobbies came down on us costers--came in a reggerlar wax,
  And them as 'ud got no license was summerned to pay the tax.
  But I had a friend among 'em, and he come in a friendly way,
  And he sez, 'You must settle your dawg, Bill, unless you've a mind to pay.'

The missus was dyin' wi' fever--I'd made a mistake in my pitch,
 I couldn't afford to keep her, so I sez, 'I'll drownd the bitch.'

 I wasn't a-goin' to lose her, I warn't such a brute, you bet,
 As to leave her to die by inches o' hunger, and cold, and wet;
 I never said now't to the missus--we both on us liked her well--
 But I takes her the follerin' Sunday down to the Grand Canell.
 I gets her tight by the collar--the Lord forgive my sin!
 And, kneelin' down on the towpath, I ducks the poor beast in.
 She gave just a sudden whine like, then a look comes into her eyes
 As 'ull last forever in mine, sir, up to the day I dies.

 And a chill came over my heart then, and thinkin' I heard her moan,
 I held her below the water, beating her skull with a stone.
 You can see the mark of it now, sir--that place on the top of 'er 'ed--
 And sudden she ceased to struggle, and I fancied as she was dead.
 I shall never know how it happened, but goin' to lose my hold,
 My knees slipped over the towpath, and into the stream I rolled;

The Dog In Action

  Down like a log I went, sir, and my eyes were filled with mud,
    And the water was tinged above me with a murdered creeter's blood.

  I gave myself up for lost then, and I cursed in my wild despair,
    And sudden I rose to the surfis, and a su'thing grabbed at my hair,
    Grabbed at my hair and loosed it, and grabbed me agin by the throat,
    And she was a-holdin' my 'ed up, and somehow I kep' afloat.
  I can't tell yer 'ow she done it, for I never knowed no more
    Till somebody seized my collar, and give me a lug ashore;
    And my head was queer and dizzy, but I see as the bitch was weak,
    And she lay on her side a-pantin', waitin' for me to speak.

  What did I do with her, eh? You'd a-hardly need to ax,
    But I sold my barrer a Monday, and paid the bloomin' tax.
    That's right, Mr. Preacher, pat her--you ain't not afeared of her now!--
    Dang this here tellin' of stories--look at the muck on my brow.

  I'm weaker, an' weaker, an' weaker; I fancy the end ain't fur,

But you know why here on my deathbed I think o' the Lord and her,
   And he who, by men's hands tortured, uttered that prayer divine,
   'Ull pardon me linkin' him like with a dawg as forgave like mine.
   When the Lord in his mercy calls me to my last eternal pitch,
   I know as you'll treat her kindly--promise to take my bitch!

   GEORGE R. SIMS.

THE DOG OF THE LOUVRE

With gentle tread, with uncovered head,
   Pass by the Louvre gate,
Where buried lie the "men of July,"
And flowers are hung by the passers-by,
   And the dog howls desolate.

That dog had fought in the fierce onslaught,
   Had rushed with his master on,
And both fought well;
But the master fell,

The Dog In Action

And behold the surviving one!

By his lifeless clay,
Shaggy and gray,
  His fellow-warrior stood;
Nor moved beyond,
But mingled fond
  Big tears with his master's blood.

Vigil he keeps
By those green heaps
  That tell where heroes lie.
No passer-by
Can attract his eye,
  For he knows it is not He!

At the dawn, when dew
Wets the garlands new
  That are hung in this place of mourning,
He will start to meet
The coming feet
  Of him whom he dreamt returning.

On the grave's wood-cross
When the chaplets toss,
  By the blast of midnight shaken,
How he howleth! hark!
From that dwelling dark
  The slain he would fain awaken.

When the snow comes fast

Dog Poems

On the chilly blast,
  Blanching the bleak church-yard,
With limbs outspread
On the dismal bed
  Of his liege, he still keeps guard.

Oft in the night,
With main and might,
  He strives to raise the stone;
Short respite takes:
"If master wakes,
  He'll call me," then sleeps on.

Of bayonet blades,
Of barricades,
  And guns he dreams the most;
Starts from his dream,
And then would seem
  To eye a pleading ghost.

He'll linger there
In sad despair
  And die on his master's grave.
His home?--'tis known
To the dead alone,--
  He's the dog of the nameless brave!

Give a tear to the dead,
And give some bread
  To the dog of the Louvre gate!
Where buried lie the men of July,

And flowers are hung by the passers-by,
  And the dog howls desolate.

-RALPH CECIL.

THE CHASE

Huntsman, take heed; they stop in full career.
Yon crowding flock, that at a distance gaze,
Have haply foil'd the turf. See that old hound!
How busily he works, but dares not trust
His doubtful sense; draws yet a wider ring.
Hark! Now again the chorus fills. As bells,
Sally'd awhile, at once their paean renew,
And high in air the tuneful thunder rolls,
See how they toss, with animated rage
Recovering all they lost! That eager haste
Some doubling wile foreshows. Ah! Yet once more

They're checked, hold back with speed--on either hand
They flourish round--e'en yet persist--'tis right.
Away they spring. The rustling stubbles bend
Beneath the driving storm. Now the poor chase
Begins to flag, to her last shifts reduced.
From brake to brake she flies, and visits all
Her well-known haunts, where once she ranged secure,
With love and plenty blest. See! There she goes,

She reels along, and by her gait betrays
Her inward weakness. See how black she looks!
The sweat, that clogs the obstructed pores, scarce leaves
A languid scent. And now in open view
See! See! She flies! Each eager hound exerts
His utmost speed, and stretches every nerve;
How quick she turns! Their gaping jaws eludes,
And yet a moment lives--till, round enclosed
By all the greedy pack, with infant screams
She yields her breath, and there, reluctant, dies.

  -LORD SOMERVILLE.

THE UNDER DOG

I know that the world, the great big world,
  Will never a moment stop
To see which dog may be in the fault,
  But will shout for the dog on top.
But for me, I shall never pause to ask
  Which dog may be in the right,
For my heart will beat, while it beats at all,
  For the under dog in the fight.

  -ANONYMOUS.

THE SHEPHERD AND HIS DOG

My dog and I are both grown old;
  On these wild downs we watch all day;
He looks in my face when the wind blows cold,
  And thus methinks I hear him say:

The gray stone circlet is below,
  The village smoke is at our feet;
We nothing hear but the sailing crow,
  And wandering flocks that roam and bleat.

Far off, the early horseman hies,
  In shower or sunshine rushing on;
Yonder the dusty whirlwind flies;
  The distant coach is seen and gone.

Though solitude around is spread,
  Master, alone thou shalt not be;
And when the turf is on thy head,
  I only shall remember thee.

I marked his look of faithful care,
  I placed my hand on his shaggy side;
"There is a sun that shines above,
  A sun that shines on both," I cried.

-WILLIAM LISLE BOWLES.

BETH GELERT

The spearman heard the bugle sound,
  And cheerily smiled the morn;
And many a brach, and many a hound,
  Attend Llewellyn's horn:

And still he blew a louder blast,
  And gave a louder cheer:
"Come, Gelert! Why art thou the last
  Llewellyn's horn to hear?

"Oh, where does faithful Gelert roam?
  The flower of all his race!
So true, so brave, a lamb at home,
  A lion in the chase!"

In sooth, he was a peerless hound,
  The gift of royal John,
But now no Gelert could be found,
  And all the chase rode on.

And now, as over rocks and dells,
  The gallant chidings rise,
All Snowdon's craggy chaos yells
  With many mingled cries.

That day Llewellyn little loved
  The chase of hart or hare,
And small and scant the booty proved,

The Dog In Action

For Gelert was not there.

Unpleased, Llewellyn homeward hied,
　When near the portal-seat,
His truant Gelert he espied,
　Bounding his lord to meet.

But when he gained the castle door,
　Aghast the chieftain stood;
The hound was smeared with gouts of gore,
　His lips and fangs ran blood.

Llewellyn gazed with wild surprise,
　Unused such looks to meet;
His favorite checked his joyful guise,
　And crouched and licked his feet.

Onward in haste Llewellyn passed,
　And on went Gelert, too,
And still, where'er his eyes were cast,
　Fresh blood-gouts shocked his view.

O'erturned his infant's bed he found,
　The blood-stained covert rent;
And all around, the walls and ground,
　With recent blood besprent.

He called the child--no voice replied;
　He searched, with terror wild;
Blood! Blood! He found on every side,
　But nowhere found the child!

Dog Poems

"Hell-hound! By thee my child's devoured!"
  The frantic father cried;
And to the hilt his vengeful sword
  He plunged in Gelert's side.

His suppliant, as to earth he fell,
  No pity could impart,
But still his Gelert's dying yell
  Passed heavy o'er his heart.

Aroused by Gelert's dying yell,
  Some slumberer wakened nigh;
What words the parent's joy can tell
  To hear his infant cry!

Concealed beneath a mangled heap
  His hurried search had missed,
All glowing from his rosy sleep,
  His cherub-boy he kissed.

Nor scratch had he, nor harm, nor dread,
  But, the same couch beneath,
Lay a great wolf, all torn and dead--
  Tremendous still in death.

Ah! What was then Llewellyn's pain!
  For now the truth was clear:
The gallant hound the wolf had slain
  To save Llewellyn's heir.

The Dog In Action

Vain, vain was all Llewellyn's woe;
  "Best of thy kind, adieu!
The frantic deed which laid thee low
  This heart shall ever rue!"

And now a gallant tomb they raise,
  With costly sculpture decked,
And marbles, storied with his praise,
  Poor Gelert's bones protect.

Here never could the spearman pass,
  Or forester, unmoved!
Here oft the tear-besprinkled grass
  Llewellyn's sorrow proved.

And here he hung his horn and spear,
  And oft, as evening fell,
In fancy's piercing sounds would hear
  Poor Gelert's dying yell.

  -WILLIAM ROBERT SPENCER.

THE FLAG AND THE FAITHFUL

(A Washington woman has made a loud outcry to the Secretary of

War to reprimand the soldiers at the Government Aviation Station
for burying their faithful dog, Muggsie, wrapped in the Stars
and Stripes.)

Ah, Muggsie, good and faithful dog,
    Gone to your rest!
You served your country and your flag
    The very best
That lay within your humble power,
    And in that far
Have been much better than some men
    And women are.
As you had lived, good dog, you died,
    And it is meet
The flag you served your best should be
    Your winding sheet.

-WILLIAM J. LAMPTON.

A GUARDIAN AT THE GATE

The dog beside the threshold lies,
Mocking sleep with half-shut eyes--
With head crouched down upon his feet,

The Dog In Action

Till strangers pass his sunny seat--
Then quick he pricks his ears to hark
And bustles up to growl and bark;
While boys in fear stop short their song,
And sneak in startled speed along;
And beggar, creeping like a snail,
To make his hungry hopes prevail
O'er the warm heart of charity,
Leaves his lame halt and hastens by.

-JOHN CLARE.

A TALE OF THE REIGN OF TERROR

'Twas in a neighboring land what time
  The Reign of Terror triumphed there,
And every horrid shape of crime
  Stalked out from murder's bloody lair.

'Twas in those dreadful times there dwelt
  In Lyons, the defiled with blood,
A loyal family that felt
  The earliest fury of the flood.

Wife, children, friends, it swept away
  From wretched Valrive, one by one,
Himself severely doomed to stay
  Till everything he loved was gone.

Dog Poems

A man proscribed, whom not to shun
  Was danger, almost fate, to brave,
So all forsook him, all save one--
  One faithful, humble, powerless slave.

His dog, old Nina. She had been,
  When they were boys, his children's mate,
His gallant Claude, his mild Eugene,
  Both gone before him to their fate.

They spurned her off--but evermore,
  Surmounting e'en her timid nature,
Love brought her to the prison door,
  And there she crouched, fond, faithful creature!

Watching so long, so piteously,
  That e'en the jailor--man of guilt,
Of rugged heart--was moved to cry,
  "Poor wretch, there enter if thou wilt."

And who than Nina more content
  When she had gained that dreary cell
Where lay in helpless dreariment
  The master loved so long and well?

And when into his arms she leapt
  In her old fond, familiar way,
And close into his bosom crept,
  And licked his face--a feeble ray

The Dog In Action

Of something--not yet comfort--stole
  Upon his heart's stern misery,
And his lips moved, "Poor loving fool!
  Then all have not abandoned me."

The hour by grudging kindness spared
  Expired too soon--the friends must part--
And Nina from the prison gazed,
  With lingering pace and heavy heart.

Shelter, and rest, and food she found
  With one who, for the master's sake,
Though grim suspicion stalked around,
  Dared his old servant home to take.

Beneath that friendly roof, each night
  She stayed, but still returning day--
Ay, the first beam of dawning light
  Beheld her on her anxious way.

Towards the prison, there to await
  The hour when through that dismal door
The keeper, half compassionate,
  Should bid her enter as before.

And well she seemed to comprehend
  The time appointed for her stay,
The little hour that with her friend
  She tarried there was all her day.

At last the captive's summons came;

Dog Poems

They led him forth his doom to hear;
No tremor shook his thrice-nerved frame
  Whose heart was dead to hope and fear.

So with calm step he moved along,
  And calmly faced the murderous crew,
But close and closer for the throng,
  Poor Nina to her master drew.

And she has found a resting place
  Between his knees--her old safe home--
And she looks round in every face
  As if to read his written doom.

'Twas but a step in those dread days
  From trial to the guillotine;
A moment, and Valrive surveys
  With steadfast eye the fell machine.

He mounts the platform, takes his stand
  Before the fatal block, and kneels
In preparation--but his hand
  A soft warm touch that moment feels.

His eyes glance downward, and a tear--
  The last tear they shall ever shed--
Falls as he utters, "Thou still here!"
  Upon his faithful servant's head.

Yes, she is there; that hellish shout,
  That deadly stroke, she hears them plain,

The Dog In Action

And from the headless trunk starts out
  Even over her the bloody rain.

Old faithful Nina! There lies she,
  Her cold head on the cold earth pressed,
As it was wont so lovingly
  To lie upon her master's breast.

And there she stayed the livelong day,
  Mute, motionless, her sad watch keeping;
A stranger who had passed that way
  Would have believed her dead or sleeping.

But if a step approached the grave
  Her eye looked up with jealous care,
Imploringly, as if to crave
  That no rude foot should trample there.

That night she came not, as of late,
  To her old, charitable home;
The next day's sun arose and set,
  Night fell--and still she failed to come.

Then the third day her pitying host
  Went kindly forth to seek his guest,
And found her at her mournful post,
  Stretched quietly as if at rest.

Yet she was not asleep nor dead,
  And when her master's friend she saw,
The poor old creature raised her head,

Dog Poems

And moaned, and moved one feeble paw.

But stirred not thence--and all in vain
  He called, caressed her, would have led--
Tried threats--then coaxing words again--
  Brought food--she turned away her head.

So with kind violence at last
  He bore her home with gentle care;
In her old shelter tied her fast,
  Placed food beside and left her there.

But ere the hour of rest, again
  He visited the captive's shed,
And there the cord lay, gnawed in twain--
  The food untasted--she was fled.

And, vexed, he cried, "Perverse old creature!
  Well, let her go. I've done my best."
But there was something in his nature,
  A feeling that would not let him rest.

So with the early light once more
  Toward the burial ground went he;
And there he found her as before,
  But not, as then, stretched quietly.

For she had worked the long night through,
  In the strong impulse of despair,
Down, down into the grave--and now,
  Panting and weak, still laboured there.

The Dog In Action

But death's cold, stiffening frost benumbs
  Her limbs, and clouds her heavy eye--
And hark! her feeble moan becomes
  A shriek of human agony.

As if before her task was over
  She feared to die in her despair.
But see! those last faint strokes uncover
  A straggling lock of thin grey hair.

One struggle, one convulsive start,
  And there the face beloved lies--
Now be at peace, thou faithful heart!
  She licks the livid lips, and dies.

-CAROLINE BOWLES SOUTHEY.

AN ELEGY ON THE DEATH OF A MAD DOG

Good people all, of every sort,
  Give ear unto my song,
And if you find it wond'rous short,
  It cannot hold you long.

In Islington there was a man

Dog Poems

Of whom the world might say
That still a godly race he ran
　Whene'er he went to pray.

A kind and gentle heart he had,
　To comfort friends and foes;
The naked every day he clad
　When he put on his clothes.

And in that town a dog was found,
　As many dogs there be,
Both mongrel, puppy, whelp and hound,
　And curs of low degree.

The dog and man at first were friends,
　But when a pique began,
The dog, to gain some private ends,
　Went mad, and bit the man.

Around from all the neighboring streets
　The wondering neighbors ran,
And swore the dog had lost his wits,
　To bite so good a man.

The wound it seem'd both sore and sad
　To every Christian eye;
And while they swore the dog was mad,
　They swore the man would die.

But soon a wonder came to light,
　That showed the rogues they lied;

The man recover'd of the bite,
  The dog it was that died.

-OLIVER GOLDSMITH.

THE FUSILIERS' DOG

Go lift him gently from the wheels,
  And soothe his dying pain,
For love and care e'en yet he feels
  Though love and care be vain;
'Tis sad that, after all these years,
  Our comrade and our friend,
The brave dog of the Fusiliers,
  Should meet with such an end.

Up Alma's hill, among the vines,
  We laughed to see him trot,
Then frisk along the silent lines
  To chase the rolling shot;
And, when the work waxed hard by day,
  And hard and cold by night,
When that November morning lay
  Upon us, like a blight;

And eyes were strained, and ears were bent,
  Against the muttering north,

Dog Poems

Till the gray mist took shape and sent
  Gray scores of Russians forth--
Beneath that slaughter wild and grim
  Nor man nor dog would run;
He stood by us, and we by him,
  Till the great fight was done.

And right throughout the snow and frost
  He faced both shot and shell;
Though unrelieved, he kept his post,
  And did his duty well.
By death on death the time was stained,
  By want, disease, despair;
Like autumn leaves our army waned,
  But still the dog was there.

He cheered us through those hours of gloom;
  We fed him in our dearth;
Through him the trench's living tomb
  Rang loud with reckless mirth;
And thus, when peace returned once more,
  After the city's fall,
That veteran home in pride we bore,
  And loved him, one and all.

With ranks re-filled, our hearts were sick,
  And to old memories clung;
The grim ravines we left glared thick
  With death-stones of the young.
Hands which had patted him lay chill,
  Voices which called were dumb,

The Dog In Action

And footsteps that he watched for still
  Never again could come.

Never again; this world of woe
  Still hurries on so fast;
They come not back; 'tis he must go
  To join them in the past.
There, with brave names and deeds entwined,
  Which Time may not forget,
Young Fusiliers unborn shall find
  The legend of our pet.

Whilst o'er fresh years and other life
  Yet in God's mystic urn
The picture of the mighty strife
  Arises sad and stern--
Blood all in front, behind far shrines
  With women weeping low,
For whom each lost one's fane but shines,
  As shines the moon on snow--

Marked by the medal, his of right,
  And by his kind, keen face,
Under that visionary light
  Poor Bob shall keep his place;
And never may our honored Queen
  For love and service pay
Less brave, less patient, or more mean
  Than his we mourn today!

-FRANCIS DOYLE.

FIDELITY

A barking sound the shepherd hears,
A cry as of a dog or fox;
He halts, and searches with his eyes
Among the scattered rocks;
And now at distance can discern
A stirring in a brake of fern,
And instantly a dog is seen,
Glancing through that covert green.

The dog is not of mountain breed,
Its motions, too, are wild and shy,
With something, as the shepherd thinks,
Unusual in its cry.
Nor is there anyone in sight,
All round, in hollow or on height,
Nor shout nor whistle strikes his ear.
What is the creature doing here?

It was a cove, a huge recess
That keeps, till June, December's snow;
A lofty precipice in front,
A silent tarn below.
Far in the bosom of Helvellyn,
Remote from public road or dwelling,
Pathway, or cultivated land,
From trace of human foot or hand.

There sometimes doth a leaping fish

The Dog In Action

Send through the tarn a lonely cheer;
The crags repeat the raven's croak
In symphony austere;
Thither the rainbow comes--the cloud,
And mists that spread the flying shroud,
And sunbeams, and the sounding blast,
That, if it could, would hurry past,
But that enormous barrier binds it fast.

Not free from boding thoughts, a while
The shepherd stood; then makes his way
Towards the dog, o'er rocks and stones,
As quickly as he may;
Nor far had gone before he found
A human skeleton on the ground;
The appalled discoverer, with a sigh,
Looks round, to learn the history

From whose abrupt and perilous rocks
The man had fallen, that place of fear!
At length upon the shepherd's mind
It breaks, and all is clear:
He instantly recalled the name
And who he was, and whence he came;
Remembered, too, the very day
On which the traveller passed this way.

But hear a wonder, for whose sake
This lamentable tale I tell!
A lasting monument of words
This wonder merits well.

The dog, which still was hovering nigh,
Repeating the same timid cry--
This dog had been through three months' space
A dweller in that savage place.

Yes, proof was plain that since the day
When this ill-fated traveller died,
The dog had watched about the spot
Or by his master's side;
How nourished here through such long time
He knows who gave that love sublime,
And gave that strength of feeling, great
Above all human estimate.

-WILLIAM WORDSWORTH.

THE SHEPHERD DOG OF THE PYRENEES

Traveler. Begone, you, sir! Here, shepherd, call your dog.
 Shepherd.   Be not affrighted, madame. Poor Pierrot
 Will do no harm. I know his voice is gruff,
 But then, his heart is good.
 Traveler.   Well, call him, then.
 I do not like his looks. He's growling now.
 Shepherd. Madame had better drop that stick. Pierrot,
 He is as good a Christian as myself

The Dog In Action

  And does not like a stick.
Traveler.   Such a fierce look!
 And such great teeth!
Shepherd.   Ah, bless poor Pierrot's teeth!
 Good cause have I and mine to bless those teeth.
 Come here, my Pierrot. Would you like to hear,
 Madame, what Pierrot's teeth have done for me?
Traveler.   Torn a gaunt wolf, I'll warrant.
Shepherd.   Do you see
 On that high ledge a cross of wood that stands
 Against the sky?
Traveler.   Just where the cliff goes down
 A hundred fathoms sheer, a wall of rock
 To where the river foams along its bed?
 I've often wondered who was brave to plant
 A cross on such an edge.
Shepherd.   Myself, madame,
 That the good God might know I gave him thanks.
 One night, it was November, black and thick,
 The fog came down, when as I reached my house
 Marie came running out; our little one,
 Our four year Louis, so she cried, was lost.
 I called Pierrot: "Go, seek him, find my boy,"
 And off he went. Marie ran crying loud
 To call the neighbors. They and I, we searched
 All that dark night. I called Pierrot in vain;
 Whistled and called, and listened for his voice;
 He always came or barked at my first word,
 But now, he answered not. When day at last
 Broke, and the gray fog lifted, there I saw
 On that high ledge, against the dawning light.

My little one asleep, sitting so near
That edge that as I looked his red barette
Fell from his nodding head down the abyss.
And there, behind him, crouched Pierrot; his teeth,
His good, strong teeth, clenching the jacket brown,
Holding the child in safety. With wild bounds
Swift as the gray wolf's own I climbed the steep,
And as I reached them Pierrot beat his tail,
And looked at me, so utterly distressed,
With eyes that said: "Forgive, I could not speak,"
But never loosed his hold till my dear rogue
Was safe within my arms.
        Ah, ha, Pierrot,
Madame forgives your barking and your teeth;
I knew she would.
Traveler.   Come here, Pierrot, good dog,
Come here, poor fellow, faithful friend and true,
Come, come, be friends with me.

-ELLEN MURRAY.

THE DOG UNDER THE WAGON

"Come, wife," said good old farmer Gray,
"Put on your things, 'tis market day,
And we'll be off to the nearest town,
There and back ere the sun goes down.

The Dog In Action

Spot? No, we'll leave old Spot behind,"
But Spot he barked and Spot he whined,
And soon made up his doggish mind
      To follow under the wagon.

Away they went at a good round pace
And joy came into the farmer's face,
"Poor Spot," said he, "did want to come,
But I'm awful glad he's left at home--
He'll guard the barn, and guard the cot,
And keep the cattle out of the lot."
"I'm not so sure of that," thought Spot,
      The dog under the wagon.

The farmer all his produce sold
And got his pay in yellow gold:
Home through the lonely forest. Hark!
A robber springs from behind a tree;
"Your money or else your life," says he;
The moon was up, but he didn't see
      The dog under the wagon.

Spot ne'er barked and Spot ne'er whined
But quickly caught the thief behind;
He dragged him down in the mire and dirt,
And tore his coat and tore his shirt,
Then held him fast on the miry ground;
The robber uttered not a sound,
While his hands and feet the farmer bound,
      And tumbled him into the wagon.

So Spot he saved the farmer's life,
The farmer's money, the farmer's wife,
And now a hero grand and gay,
A silver collar he wears today;
Among his friends, among his foes--
And everywhere his master goes--
He follows on his horny toes,
      The dog under the wagon.

-ANONYMOUS.

SAL'S TOWSER AND MY TROUSER

A RUSTIC IDYL BY A RUSTIC IDLER

But yestere'en I loved thee whole,
Oh, fashionable and baggy trouser!
And now I loathe and hate the hole
In thee, I do, I trow, sir.

I sallied out to see my Sal,
Across yon round hill's brow, sir;
I didn't know she, charming gal,
Had a dog,--a trouser-browser.

I'd sauntered in quite trim and spruce,

The Dog In Action

When on a sudden, oh, my trouser,
I felt thee seized where thou'rt most loose,--
I tarried there with Towser.

I on the fence, he down below,
And thou the copula, my trouser,
I thought he never would let go,--
This gentle Towser.

They say that fashion cuts thee loose,
But not so fashioned is Sal's Towser;
Thou gavest away at last, no use
To tarry, tearèd trouser.

Miss Sarah, she is wondrous sweet,
And I'd have once loved to espouse her,
But my calling trouser has no seat,--
I left it there with Towser.

So all unseated is my suit;
I must eschew Miss Sarah now, sir;
He's chewed my trouser; 'twouldn't suit
Me to meet Towser.

   -ANONYMOUS.

ROVER IN CHURCH

'Twas a Sunday morning in early May,
A beautiful, sunny, quiet day,
And all the village, old and young,
Had trooped to church when the church bell rung.
The windows were open, and breezes sweet
Fluttered the hymn books from seat to seat.
Even the birds in the pale-leaved birch
Sang as softly as if in church!

Right in the midst of the minister's prayer
There came a knock at the door. "Who's there,
I wonder?" the gray-haired sexton thought,
As his careful ear the tapping caught.
Rap-rap, rap-rap--a louder sound,
The boys on the back seats turned around.
What could it mean? for never before
Had any one knocked at the old church door.

Again the tapping, and now so loud,
The minister paused (though his head was bowed).
Rappety-rap! This will never do,
The girls are peeping, and laughing too!
So the sexton tripped o'er the creaking floor,
Lifted the latch and opened the door.

In there trotted a big black dog,
As big as a bear! With a solemn jog
Right up the centre aisle he pattered;

The Dog In Action

People might stare, it little mattered.
Straight he went to a little maid,
Who blushed and hid, as though afraid,
And there sat down, as if to say,
"I'm sorry that I was late today,
But better late than never, you know;
Beside, I waited an hour or so,
And couldn't get them to open the door
Till I wagged my tail and bumped the floor.
Now little mistress, I'm going to stay,
And hear what the minister has to say."

The poor little girl hid her face and cried!
But the big dog nestled close to her side,
And kissed her, dog fashion, tenderly,
Wondering what the matter could be!
The dog being large (and the sexton small),
He sat through the sermon, and heard it all,
As solemn and wise as any one there,
With a very dignified, scholarly air!
And instead of scolding, the minister said,
As he laid his hand on the sweet child's head,
After the service, "I never knew
Two better list'ners than Rover and you!"

-JAMES BUCKHAM.

4

The Dog's Hereafter

Oh, Indra, and what of this dog? It hath faithfully followed me through;
 Let it go with me into Heaven, for my soul is full of compassion.

The Dog's Hereafter

BILLY

Dear Billy, of imperious bark
　When stranger's step fell on thy ear;
　Who oft inspired with wholesome fear
A prowling boy in shadows dark:

But oftener hailed with joyous cry
　Some friendly face returning home,
　Or, wild with glee, the fields to roam--
Now still and cold thou here dost lie!

Frail vines that from the garden wall
　Crept blooming o'er thy lowly bed,
　Elm branches drooping overhead,
And dying leaves that wavering fall,

In other forms of life enrolled
　Shall live in ages yet to be;
　And shall a mind from body free
Lie buried dark beneath the mold?

He loved us all, and none forgot,
　He guessed whate'er was done or told,
　Dreamed of adventures free and bold--
For him is there no future lot?

If love is life and thought is mind,
　And all shall last beyond the years,
　And memory live in other spheres,

My steadfast friend may I not find?

-LORENZO SEARS.

THE BOND

When I call my terrier by his name,
  Or join him at evening play;
His eyes will flash with a human flame
  And he looks what he cannot say;
For the bond between us two
Is that between me and you!

Should a seraph sing in my ear tonight,
  Or a sweet voiced angel come.
Would poor speech prove my soul's delight,
  Or ecstasy drive me dumb?
For the link 'twixt them and me
Is long as Eternity.

Wide leagues our sentient forms divide
  The loftier from the mean;
But soul to soul all planes are tied
  When sympathy lies between;
And who shall say that the brute
Is soulless, though mean and mute?

-GEORGE H. NETTLE.

The Dog's Hereafter

TO A DOG

On every side I see your trace;
  Your water-trough's scarce dry;
Your empty collar in its place
  Provokes the heavy sigh.

And you were here two days ago.
  There's little changed, I see.
The sun is just as bright, but oh!
  The difference to me!

The very print of your small pad
  Is on the whitened stone.
Where, by what ways, or sad or glad,
  Do you fare on alone?

Oh, little face, so merry-wise,
  Brisk feet and eager bark!
The house is lonesome for your eyes,
  My spirit somewhat dark.

Now, small, invinc'ble friend, your love
  Is done, your fighting o'er,
No more your wandering feet will rove
  Beyond your own house-door.

The cats that feared, their hearts are high,
  The dogs that loved will gaze
Long, long ere you come passing by

With all your jovial ways.

Th' accursed archer who has sent
  His arrow all too true,
Would that his evil days were spent
  Ere he took aim at you!

Your honest face, your winsome ways
  Haunt me, dear little ghost,
And everywhere I see your trace,
  Oh, well-beloved and lost!

-ANONYMOUS.

CANINE IMMORTALITY

And they have drowned thee then at last! poor Phillis!
The burden of old age was heavy on thee,
And yet thou shouldst have lived! What though thine eye
Was dim, and watched no more with eager joy
The wonted call that on thy dull sense sunk
With fruitless repetition, the warm sun
Might still have cheered thy slumber; thou didst love
To lick the hand that fed thee, and though past
Youth's active season, even life itself
Was comfort. Poor old friend! How earnestly
Would I have pleaded for thee! thou hadst been

The Dog's Hereafter

Still the companion of my childish sports:
And as I roamed o'er Avon's woody cliffs,
From many a day-dream has thy short quick bark
Recalled my wandering soul. I have beguiled
Often the melancholy hours at school,
Soured by some little tyrant, with the thought
Of distant home, and I remembered then
Thy faithful fondness: for not mean the joy,
Returning at the pleasant holidays,
I felt from thy dumb welcome. Pensively
Sometimes have I remarked the slow decay,
Feeling myself changed, too, and musing much,
On many a sad vicissitude of life!
Ah, poor companion! when thou followedst last
Thy master's parting footsteps to the gate
Which closed forever on him, thou didst lose
Thy truest friend, and none was left to plead
For the old age of brute fidelity!
But fare thee well! Mine is no narrow creed;
And He who gave thee being did not frame
The mystery of life to be the sport
Of merciless man! There is another world
For all that live and move--a better one!
Where the proud bipeds, who would fain confine
Infinite goodness to the little bounds
Of their own charity, may envy thee!

-ROBERT SOUTHEY.

A FRIENDLY WELCOME

'Tis sweet to hear the watch-dog's honest bark
  Bay deep-mouthed welcome as we draw near home;
'Tis sweet to know there is an eye will mark
  Our coming, and look brighter when we come.

  -LORD BYRON.

EXEMPLARY NICK

Here lies poor Nick, an honest creature,
Of faithful, gentle, courteous nature;
A parlor pet unspoiled by favor,
A pattern of good dog behavior,
Without a wish, without a dream,
Beyond his home and friends at Cheam.
Contentedly through life he trotted,
Along the path that faith allotted,
Till time, his aged body wearing,
Bereaved him of his sight and hearing,
Then laid him down without a pain
To sleep, and never wake again.

  -SYDNEY SMITH.

The Dog's Hereafter

THE DIFFERENCE

My dog! The difference between thee and me
Knows only our Creator--only he
Can number the degrees in being's scale
Between th' Instinctive lamp, ne'er known to fail,
And that less steady light, of brighter ray,
The soul which animates thy master's clay;
And he alone can tell by what fond tie
My look thy life, my death thy sign to die.

No, when that feeling quits thy glazing eye
'Twill live in some blest world beyond the sky.

-ANONYMOUS.

LADDIE

Lowly the soul that waits
At the white, celestial gates,
A threshold soul to greet
Belovéd feet.

Down the streets that are beams of sun
Cherubim children run;
They welcome it from the wall;

Their voices call.

But the Warder saith: "Nay, this
Is the City of Holy Bliss.
What claim canst thou make good
To angelhood?"

"Joy," answereth it from eyes
That are amber ecstasies,
Listening, alert, elate,
Before the gate.

> Oh, how the frolic feet
> On lonely memory beat!
> What rapture in a run
> 'Twixt snow and sun!

"Nay, brother of the sod,
What part hast thou in God?
What spirit art thou of?"
It answers: "Love."

Lifting its head, no less
Cajoling a caress,
Our winsome collie wraith,
Than in glad faith.

The door will open wide,
Or kind voice bid: "Abide,
A threshold soul to greet
The longed-for feet."

The Dog's Hereafter

Ah, Keeper of the Portal,
If Love be not immortal,
If Joy be not divine,
What prayer is mine?

-KATHERINE LEE BATES.

A DOG'S EPITAPH

When some proud son of man returns to earth,
Unknown to glory, but upheld by birth,
The sculptor's art exhausts the pomp of wo,
And storied urns record who rests below;
When all is done, upon the tomb is seen
Not what he was, but what he should have been,
But the poor dog, in life the firmest friend,
The first to welcome, foremost to defend,
Whose honest heart is still his master's own,
Who labors, fights, lives, breathes for him alone,

Unhonored falls, unnoticed all his worth,
Denied in Heaven the soul he held in earth;
While man, vain insect! hopes to be forgiven,
And claims himself a sole, exclusive Heaven.
Oh, man! thou feeble tenant of an hour,
Debased by slavery or corrupt by power,

Who knows thee well must quit thee with disgust,
Degraded mass of animated dust!

Thy love is lust, thy friendship all a cheat,
Thy smiles hypocrisy, thy words deceit!
By nature vile, ennobled but by name,
Each kindred brute might bid thee blush for shame.
Ye! who perchance behold this simple urn,
Pass on--it honors none you wish to mourn;
To mark a friend's remains these stones arise--
I never knew but one, and here he lies.

-LORD BYRON.

THE PASSING OF A DOG

This kindly friend of mine who's passed
  Beyond the realm of day,
Beyond the realm of darkling night,
  To unknown bourne away

Was one who deemed my humble home
  A palace grand and fair;
Whose fullest joy it was to find
  His comrade ever there.

Ah! He has gone from out my life

The Dog's Hereafter

Like some dear dream I knew.
A man may own a hundred dogs,
  But one he loves, and true.

-ANONYMOUS.

MY DOG

The curate thinks you have no soul!
  I know that he has none. But you,
Dear friend! whose solemn self-control
  In our four-square, familiar pew,

Was pattern to my youth--whose bark
  Called me in summer dawns to rove--
Have you gone down into the dark
  Where none is welcome, none may love?

I will not think those good brown eyes
  Have spent their light of truth so soon;
But in some canine Paradise
  Your wraith, I know, rebukes the moon,

And quarters every plain and hill
  Seeking its master. As for me,
This prayer at least the gods fulfill--
  That when I pass the floor, and see

Old Charon by the Stygian coast
  Take toll of all the shades who land,
Your little, faithful, barking ghost
  May leap to lick my phantom hand.

  -ANONYMOUS.

JACK

Dog Jack has gone on the silent trail,
  Wherever that may be;
But well I know, when I whistle the call,
  He will joyfully answer me.

That call will be when I, myself,
  Have passed through the Gates of Gold;
He will come with a rush, and his soft brown eyes
  Will glisten with love as of old.

Oh, Warder of Gates, in the far-away land,
  This little black dog should you see,
Throw wide your doors that this faithful friend
  May enter, and wait for me.

  -H.P.W.

The Dog's Hereafter

IN MEMORY OF "DON"

Our Don--only a dog!
Yes, only a dog, you say;
With a large, warm heart,
And a bright, brown eye,
With an earnest bark
And a warm caress

For you and me and
The friends he loved best.
Oh, how we shall
Miss him, you and I,
His noisy welcome, and
Rough good-bye!

Some time, somewhere,
Some day, I trust,
We shall meet again;
Oh, yes, we must!
And the joy of that meeting
I dare not say.

Ay, mock, ye skeptics,
And laugh to scorn
The faith I hold
Of all life that's born;
It cannot be wasted,
Nor can it be lost.

And oh, for the faith,
And the Indian's trust,
That Don and his mistress
Will meet some day--
Just over the river
Not far away!

  -M.S.W.

RODERICK DHU

You are just a poor dumb brute, my Roderick Dhu,
And our scientific brethren scoff at you.
They "reason" and they "think,"
Then they set it down in ink,
And clinch it with their learned "point of view."

Even some divines deny you have a soul,
And reject you from Man's final heav'nly goal:
Your presence isn't wanted
You're not of the anointed.
You're not upon the mighty Judgment Roll.

Yet the truth shines from your eyes, my faithful friend,
And your faithfulness doth that of men transcend;
You would lie right down and die,
Without even wond'ring why,

The Dog's Hereafter

To save the man you loved--and meet your end.

When my heart was almost breaking, Roderick Dhu,
Who was it gave me sympathy, but you!
You crept so close to me,
And you licked me tenderly,
And not a human friend was half so true.

And would I, reasoning wisely, pronounce you just a beast?
Your actions "automatic," not "conscious" in the least?
Set myself so high above you,
As not to know and love you,
And toss you but a bone while I shall feast?

My bonnie Collie, such wrong there shall not be,
Not for me to grasp at Heav'n and leave the Dark for thee,
You're nothing but a dog,
Not in Heaven's Catalogue--
But whatsoe'er thy fate, the same for me.

-HELEN FITZGERALD SANDERS.

QUESTIONS

  Where are you now, little wandering
Life, that so faithfully dwelt with us,
Played with us, fed with us, felt with us,
  Years we grew fonder and fonder in?

  You who but yesterday sprang to us,
Are we forever bereft of you?
And is this all that is left of you--
  One little grave, and a pang to us?

-WILLIAM HURRELL MALLOCK.

HIS EPITAPH

His friends he loves. His fellest earthly foes--
Cats--I believe he did but feign to hate.
My hand will miss the insinuated nose,
Mine eyes the tail that wagged contempt at Fate.

-WILLIAM WATSON.

The Dog's Hereafter

IN MEMORIAM

I miss the little wagging tail;
I miss the plaintive, pleading wail;
I miss the wistful, loving glance;
I miss the circling welcome-dance.

I miss the eyes that, watching, sued;
I miss her tongue of gratitude
That licked my hand, in loving mood,
When we divided cup or food.

I miss the pertinacious scratch
(Continued till I raised the latch
Each morning), waiting at my door;
Alas, I ne'er shall hear it more.

"What folly!" hints the cynic mind,
"Plenty of dogs are left behind
To snap and snarl, to bark and bite,
And wake us in the gloomy night.

"You should have sought a human friend,
Whose life eternal ne'er could end--
Whose gifts of intellect and grace
Bereavement never could efface."

Plenty of snarling things are left,
But I am of a friend bereft;
I seek not intellect, but heart--

Dog Poems

'Tis not my head that feels the smart.

While loving sympathy is cherished,
While gratitude is not quite perished;
While patient, hopeful, cheerful meeting
At our return is pleasant greeting;

So long my heart will feel a void--
Grieving, my mind will be employed--
When I, returning to my door,
Shall miss what I shall find no more.

When we, at last, shall pass away,
And see no more the light of day,
Will many hearts as vacant mourn--
As truly wish for our return?

Yet love that's true will ever know
The pain of parting. Better so!
"Better to love and lose" than cold,
And colder still, let hearts grow old.

So let the cynic snarl or smile,
And his great intellect beguile;
My little dog, so true to me,
Will dear to heart and memory be.

 -HENRY WILLETT.

QUESTIONS

Is there not something in the pleading eye
Of the poor brute that suffers, which arraigns
The law that bids it suffer? Has it not
A claim for some remembrance in the book
That fills its pages with the idle words
Spoken of man? Or is it only clay,
Bleeding and aching in the potter's hand,
Yet all his own to treat it as he will,
And when he will to cast it at his feet,
Shattered, dishonored, lost for evermore?
My dog loves me, but could he look beyond
His earthly master, would his love extend
To Him who--hush! I will not doubt that He
Is better than our fears, and will not wrong
The least, the meanest of created things.

-OLIVER WENDELL HOLMES.

OUR DOG JOCK

A rollicksome, frolicsome, rare old cock
As ever did nothing was our dog Jock;
A gleesome, fleasome, affectionate beast,
As slow at a fight as swift at a feast;

A wit among dogs, when his life 'gan fail,
One couldn't but see the old wag in his tail,
When his years grew long and his eyes grew dim,
And his course of bark could not strengthen him.
Never more now shall our knees be pressed
By his dear old chops in their slobbery rest,
Nor our mirth be stirred at his solemn looks,
As wise, and as dull, as divinity books.
Our old friend's dead, but we all well know
He's gone to the Kennels where the good dogs go,
Where the cooks be not, but the beef-bones be,
And his old head never need turn for a flea.

-JAMES PAYN.

TORY, A PUPPY

He lies in the soft earth under the grass,
Where they who love him often pass,
And his grave is under a tall young lime,
In whose boughs the pale green hop-flowers climb;
But his spirit--where does his spirit rest?
It was God who made him--God knows best.

-MORTIMER COLLINS.

The Dog's Hereafter

ON AN IRISH RETRIEVER

Ten years of loving loyalty
  Unthankéd should not go to earth,
And I, who had no less from thee,
  Devote this tribute to thy worth.

For thou didst give to me, old friend,
  Thy service while thy life did last;
Thy life and service have an end,
  And here I thank thee for the past.

Trusted and faithful, tried and true,
  Watchful and swift to do my will,
Grateful for care that was thy due,
  To duty's call obedient still,

From ill thou knew'st thou didst refrain,
  The good thou knew'st thou strove to do,
Nor dream of fame, nor greed of gain,
  Man's keenest spurs, urged thee thereto.

Brute, with a heart of human love,
  And speechless soul of instinct fine!
How few by reason's law who move
  Deserve an epitaph like thine!

-FANNY KEMBLE BUTLER.

A RETRIEVER'S EPITAPH

Beneath this turf, that formerly he pressed
With agile feet, a dog is laid to rest;
Him, as he sleeps, no well-known sound shall stir,
The rabbit's patter, or the pheasant's whir;
The keeper's "Over"--far, but well defined,
That speeds the startled partridge down the wind;
The whistled warning as the winged ones rise
Large and more large upon our straining eyes,
Till with a sweep, while every nerve is tense,
The chattering covey hurtles o'er the fence;
The double crack of every lifted gun,
The dinting thud of birds whose course is done--
These sounds, delightful to his listening ear,
He heeds no longer, for he cannot hear.
None stauncher, till the drive was done, defied
Temptation, rooted to his master's side;
None swifter, when his master gave the word,
Leapt on his course to track the running bird,
And bore it back--ah, many a time and oft--
His nose as faultless as his mouth was soft.
How consciously, how proudly unconcerned,
Straight to his master's side he then returned,
Wagged a glad tail, and deemed himself repaid
As in that master's hand the bird he laid,
If, while a word of praise was duly said,
The hand should stroke his smooth and honest head.
Through spring and summer, in the sportless days,
Cheerful he lived a life of simpler ways;

The Dog's Hereafter

Chose, since official dogs at times unbend,
The household cat for confidante and friend;
With children friendly, but untaught to fawn,
Romped through the walks and rollicked on the lawn,
Rejoiced, if one the frequent ball should throw,
To fetch it, scampering gaily to and fro,
Content through every change of sportive mood
If one dear voice, one only, called him good.

Such was my dog, who now, without my aid,
Hunts through the shadowland, himself a shade,
Or crouched intent before some ghostly gate,
Waits for my step, as here he used to wait.

  -ROBERT C. LEHMANN.

Dog Poems

Printed in Great Britain
by Amazon